BOY'S BOOK OF CAMPING AND WOOD CRAFTS

BOY'S BOOK OF CAMPING
AND WOOD CRAFTS

with a new introduction by Herb Gordon, author of *The Joy of Family Camping*

BERNARD S. MASON

THE DERRYDALE PRESS
Lanham and New York

THE DERRYDALE PRESS

Published in the United States of America
by The Derrydale Press
4501 Forbes Boulevard, Suite 200, Lanham, Maryland 20706

Distributed by NATIONAL BOOK NETWORK, INC.

First Derrydale Edition 2001
Introduction Copyright © 2001 by The Derrydale Press

This Derrydale Press paperback edition of *Boy's Book of Camping and Wood Crafts* is an abridged republication of the edition first published in 1939 by A. S. Barnes & Company under the title *Woodcraft*, here updated with a new introduction.

Library of Congress Cataloging-in-Publication Data
Mason, Bernard Sterling, 1896-1953.
    [Woodcraft. 1, Campcraft]
    The boy's guide to camping and wood crafts / Bernard S. Mason.
        p. cm.
    Originally published: Woodcraft. New York : A.S. Barnes & Co., 1939. With new introd.
ISBN 1-58667-072-7 (pbk. : alk. paper)
    1. Camping. I. Title.

GV191.7 .M266 2001
796.54—dc21   2001028644

⊖™ The paper used in this publication meets the minimum requirements of American National Standard for Information Sciences—Permanence of Paper for Printed Library Materials, ANSI/NISO Z39.48–1992.
Manufactured in the United States of America.

CONTENTS

INTRODUCTION

"The most beautiful and colorful movable home in all the world is the tepee of the plains." With this commentary on the traditional dwelling of Native Americans, Bernard S. Mason illustrates not only his deep admiration of them as a people but provides a unique review of the variety of dwellings they built before the arrival of Europeans.

But there is far more to *Boy's Book to Camping and Woodcraft* than recreating ancient dwellings. The author also reviews camping styles practiced before World War II when outdoor travelers were far less ecologically aware of the critical need for conservation than those who head for the woodlands today. He reviews the clothing, shoes, tents and campfire gadgets they once used or wore and the critical role of good axmanship in their camps.

As for the teepees of the Native Americans, there were far more styles of housing among those peoples than conical tents. Mason notes that "as the natural environment varied, the type of shelter varied depending upon the materials, the environment and the culture of the tribes.

"Wigwams, most people seem to picture in their mind as being pointed or cone shaped . . . but the pointed style was from the most characteristic and commonly used dwelling in the northern woodlands. Rather a dome-shaped wigwam or *waginogan* (pronounced wä´ge-noo-gän´) was the permanent year-around shelter . . . the pointed bark type or *nasa-ogan* (pronounced nä´sa-o-gän´) being used only in the temporary camps during the summer months when the family was moving frequently from place to another."

TEPEES

For a moment let's concentrate on the tepee, which Mason calls the "nearest to the ideal dwelling that has ever been devised." Tepees were found across the "wide frontier of prairie-land, used alike by the Dakota, the Assiniboin, the Cheyenne, the Arapaho, the Missouri, the Omaha, and the Crow, among others."

The first summer tepees were moved from campsite to campsite by the women and dogs. They rarely were more than ten feet tall. But once horses became available to the American Indians, tepees bloomed overnight, typically to sixteen to twenty feet in height. Sometimes the size of tepees towered to even twenty-five feet high.

For those fascinated by tepees, Mason carefully and skillfully describes how to build one, complete with measurements and diagrams. Those technical descriptions of making a tepee could be followed today for a family that wants to build an unusual summer home on a distant beach. Use long commercial poles instead of chopping down and trimming trees. Or an outdoor camping facility could add a large tepee as a special meeting place for boys and girls who are in their camp for the summer. Mason also provides detailed instructions for making a permanent wigwam of sturdy branches covered with bark. But modern campers should use plastic or aluminum poles covered with sheets of heavy plastic.

LEAN-TOS

Mason illustrates how Native Americans built various styles of slab lean-tos that eventually led to the construction of the famed log Adirondack shelters, with an open front and sloping roof. These are still popular at trail campsites in many wilderness settings. He concludes his discussion on various shelters listing woods that were used in housing from those "very resistant to decay" to woods that " decay very quickly."

Mason's advice on camping styles and techniques popular before the 1940s are described in a wonderfully informative chapter on "Beds and Duffel." To Mason, our grandfather campers were broken into two distinct qroups: the innocent tenderfoot who "means well and tries hard" and the "tenderfoot No. 2." The former "hauls into the woods . . . far and away too much stuff, most of which will never be used." The latter is an outrageous braggart who "takes little or nothing" and, ignoring the reality of a tough outing, boasts of his ruggedness but only after he returns to his desk in the city.

Mason says that both types of tenderfeet, however, eventually learn how to create a comfortable camp "if they camp long enough." The former who "settles down to an outfit that is at once light and adequate," and the latter who realizes that camping is "not synonymous with roughing it."

TENTS

Tents, of course, then as now, were the city dweller's normal home in the woodlands and forests. Although Mason calls canvas tents somewhat heavy, he nevertheless recommends them, when made waterproof, rather than the newer synthetics that are edging into the camper's market.

Of the tents campers could buy, Mason recommends the "explorer's tent, high enough to stand in, with a front flap which formed a sort of extended roof above the door, which could be raised by day, or tied to the tent at night." For cold weather, Mason recommends the Baker tent, a popular model of his day because it had a large front flap that could be opened on a grim night while a small reflector fire was built in front to provide heat. Mason provides drawings of the tent as he does throughout the book with everything he describes.

BEDDING, SLEEPING BAGS AND PACKS

To enjoy a sound night's sleep, Mason describes how campers can build a comfortable bed. Even though plastic air mattresses had been developed by the 1930s, Mason did not recommend them because in cold weather they did not keep you warm unless they were covered with blankets. This is still true today, but now we have the luxury of self-filling foam pads that protect the tent dweller from cold and rocky ground.

As for sleeping bags, they were generally made by pinning blankets together. Above all, Mason advises campers to "stay away from cotton blankets." Wool was the ultimate wilderness fabric, whether for clothing or bedding.

Mason says the "old adage that a camper is known by his fires contains much of truth, no doubt, but it is nearer the fact that he is known by his packs." The small "ruck sack" is only a good idea for a hiking trip but "not suitable for the camper who must haul blankets and provisions into the woods or by paddle." In his era, Mason notes that "the most popular pack . . . is the Duluth or Northwestern. This is a large sturdy pack . . . equipped with shoulder straps and a tumpline." Because of the way modern packs are designed, either with inner or outer frames, the tumpline has virtually disappeared.

FIRE-CRAFT

Fire-craft was of special importance to Mason because in his epoch, the type of wood for building a suitable fire was an essential element of camping knowledge. Today of course, the type of wood we light is only what can be found on the ground. But in Mason's day, campers had a virtually unrestricted right to chop the best burning wood they could find. Mason's techniques for starting a fire, however, are still contemporary and popular with campers today. Even his "trench candles," for use in emergencies, are still useful. I now carry a few such wads with me when I head into the wilderness.

I found it fascinating the way Mason teaches his readers about methods of starting fires using ancient Indian friction skills, as well as a myriad of ways for cooking over an open fire without pot or pan. Bernard S. Mason's *Boy's Book to Camping and Woodcraft* is chock-a-block with fascinating and half-forgotten outdoor skills of yesterday, which make simply wonderful reading for today's campers, hikers and paddlers who both relish and protect our mountains, plains and woodlands and our rivers and lakes.

Herbert Gordon,
author of *The Joy of Family Camping*

BOY'S BOOK OF CAMPING AND WOOD CRAFTS

CHAPTER I

SHELTERS FOR THE TRAIL

SAID SOMEONE, "There is no place so dismal as the woods in rain." How the city starves the soul!

When lightning flashes and the crashing voice of the Thunderbird rocks the earth, I love to go out on the dock and watch the storm approach, there to remain until driving rain and mighty wave breaking over the dock force me ashore and to shelter. I have heard the symphony orchestras of the land, I have sat entranced before the great masters of the violin and the artists of opera, but never have I heard music that can compare to the pattering of raindrops on the tent roof! He must have been imprisoned long among city walls who fails to hear music in these, the Rain God's symphonies.

My old Indian friend came in with a fresh-cut pole to be placed where strength and endurance were needed. What kind of wood is it? "Elm, *storm-tested on the high cliff side!*" Storms—the wind and the rain—make strong all things that grow.

And yet, without adequate shelter, the woods may easily turn drab and dismal in the rain. One has no stomach for romance when drenched with rain, nor zest for beauty when shivering with cold!

Sleep in the woods—sleep that house-dwelling folks can never know! Sweet, healing, restoring rest! The cool, sweet-scented night air, close to the damp and smelly earth, fragrant with the incense of the things that grow, leading to Nature's matchless blessing—the blessing of calm, sweet sleep, the woodland's perfect rest, reviving, restoring, and making strong for the battles of life in the great tomorrow!

And yet, there is no rest—with countless hordes of mosquitoes hovering about!

The aesthetic rests on a plain, mundane foundation of ordinary creature comforts. So, too, with much of joy, health, and safety. The task of camping is to provide these comforts, any place, any time, regardless of climate, topography, vegetation—and insects. The difference between inconvenience and adventure rests right here.

We are down to the bed-rock matters of comfort when discussing shelters for the trail. Nothing save food and fire is more elemental. On the streams and trails it's different from being in permanent camps for then we must haul our shelter with us, or must fashion it each night out of materials the woodland offers. Normally we will haul it, which raises the question of tents light in weight, watertight, and insect-proof. But comes the time when we are caught in the woods without a tent and then we shall thank our woodcraft training in how emergency shelters are fashioned.

EMERGENCY SHELTERS

Of course, no one would hit the trail without shelter of some sort but once in a long while we are caught unexpectedly away from camp and are forced to throw together a shelter for the night with what we have. And what we have under such conditions usually gets down to a camp ax and materials found in the woods—browse and bark.

A Poncho Shelter

If fortunate enough to have a poncho along when nightfall catches us, the easiest way out is to lay three or four poles against a large fallen log and spread the poncho over them as in Figure 1. The ends

Figure 1. A Poncho Shelter

of the sheet may be tied to the end poles. Beware of logs that do not lie solidly on the ground, however, because annoying drafts will find their way through any openings.

A Brush Den

The most primitive and at the same time the simplest, quickest, and most practical shelter that can be tossed together in short order from materials found in the woods is shown in Figure 2. Find a young fir or hemlock with ample plumage that has branches well down to the ground. Chop this four to five feet from the ground causing it to fall so that the butt is still attached to the stump if possible; otherwise lift it and put it back on the stump. Cut out the branches on the underside and also along the top for a distance of seven feet, and stack these on the sides, tips downward, thus creating the bushy, fragrant den shown in A, Figure 2, amply large for your blankets

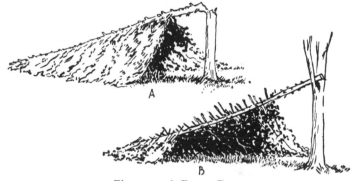

Figure 2. A Brush Den

and as watertight as any browse shelter can be expected to be. Additional branches can be cut from the unused point of the tree if necessary to reinforce the sides. In case a tree of suitable size cannot be located, cut a twenty-foot pole and lean it against a large tree, forcing one end into the rough bark about five feet up and sharpening the other end so that it can be stuck in the ground; over this lean long branches cut from bushy young firs or hemlocks to make a shelter of the same shape.

Now a shelter of this type will make a pleasant place on a night in summer but it will be cold and damp if the weather is chilly—no shelter is adequate in cold weather unless a fire can be built beside it so as to reflect heat into it. In short order, however, can we change the hemlock or fir den just described into one that will offer all the warmth a cold night will demand. This second type, pictured in B, Figure 2, is by far the better of the two models to fix in one's mind, for whether the weather is warm or cold, it fulfills every function of an emergency protection. Trim off the branches from the top, bottom and one side of the felled tree and stack them on the other side, thus forming a one-sided lean-to in front of which a roaring reflector fire can be built, warming and lighting the den and offering the cheer that the sight of dancing flames inevitably conjures up regardless of the nature of the weather.

Another cold weather device is to build a fire on the spot selected for the bed before the tree is felled, and then, after it has burned down, to scrape away the coals and ashes. When the lean-to is completed the blankets can be placed on dry, warm earth which will retain its heat under their covering well into the night.

THE THATCHED LEAN-TO

That the thatched browse lean-to is an efficient emergency shelter no one would question, but the time required to do a first-class job raises a question as to its practical value. Since the object is a night or two of protection, a shelter requiring several hours to build is

Figure 3. FRAME FOR THATCHED LEAN-TO

scarcely a common-sense undertaking—the brush den just described will fill all needs in a fraction of the time that careful thatching requires. Of course, if one must fashion a camp for several days' stay, this lean-to might be ideal, but, for that long a time, needs would normally be anticipated and shelter brought along. The emergency situation that would recommend its use would be a very cold night, for its sloping, tightly thatched roof is a

good reflector for the fire. These lean-tos are more often seen in demonstrations and displays of campcraft than in the actual life of the woods, and they do make an attractive exhibit. However, everyone should know the pattern against the emergency when it may be required.

The cross-pole of the frame may be lashed four feet from the ground to two conveniently spaced trees or placed across forked poles driven in the ground eight feet apart as in Figure 3. In case the ground is frozen so that stakes cannot be driven, and suitable trees are not handy, a tripod of three stakes tied together and placed at each end of the cross-pole will provide the support. Against this cross-bar five sticks should be leaned of such lengths that the ends resting on the ground are six feet from the uprights. In trimming these poles the stubs of all the branches should be left protruding two or three inches to provide hooks on which to rest the cross-sticks of the frame. Across these sloping poles several sticks should be placed parallel to the ridgepole, spaced a foot apart, and supported by the hooks or stubs of the trimmed branches, or lashed to the sloping end poles.

To this latticework the leafy boughs and twigs of fir, hemlock, or cedar are thatched. Beginning at the bottom and working up in layers, shingle fashion, hook the butts of the twigs under the cross-sticks with the leafy tips hanging downward and resting on the frame, so spaced that the tips cover the butts of the twigs in the row below. When the frame is all covered a good job would require starting at the bottom again giving the roof a double thatching or even a triple one—severe weather would call for a roof a foot thick. If the lean-to is to be used for some time it is well to place a row of cross-poles across the top of the browse roof to hold it firm. Cutting boughs in quantities and thatching takes time and the jobs should not be rushed.

Such a roof cannot be expected to be watertight but is excellent protection from wind and snow. It will shed the worst of the rain but there will be considerable dripping no matter how many boughs are piled on.

A QUICK LEAN-TO OF BARK

Here is the most practical lean-to for a quick camp if one is far enough back in the wilds so that the stripping of bark from standing trees, or the felling of a tree for its bark, is permissible. It can be set up in a fraction of the time required for a lean-to of boughs, is resistant to water, and reflects heat well.

No elaborate framework is necessary—merely drive two forked sticks in the ground and place a cross-pole between them as shown in Figure 4. Suitable bark may be obtained from *white cedar, spruce, basswood, hemlock, ash,* or *chestnut.* In order to get strips of the necessary length it is best to fell the tree, but before doing so lay a heavy pole on the ground near the butt to serve as a convenient skid for peeling after the log is dropped on it. Strips of bark nine feet long and a foot wide will be needed. As the bark is peeled from the tree it will spread out in broad sheets—an eight-inch tree will produce shingles of bark twenty-four inches wide—which should then be cut into narrow strips measuring approximately twelve inches. Or, and this is often the easier way, the tree may be girdled at the two points nine feet apart, and several connecting cuts made so spaced that the bark will peel off into twelve-inch widths.

First place a layer of strips lengthwise of the slope of the roof with the concave or hollow side up and then place a second layer

Figure 4. A QUICK LEAN-TO OF BARK

on top of these with the convex side up, so arranged that the edges of the upper strips rest in the troughs made by the first layer. The water will thus run into the troughs and off the roof. The roof may be made secure against the blasts of the wind by binding the bark slabs down with a strip of basswood-bark cordage (see page 220) or a rope tied to the upright poles and stretched over the bark, or by placing a pole across the bark at the top and lashing its ends to the uprights as in the drawing.

With a reflector fire in front this is a first-class shelter but a short-lived one for the heat of the sun will curl the green bark in a few days so as to ruin it.

A permanent bark lean-to is described in Chapter III.

AN INDIAN BARK KENNEL

The Menominees and Chippewas, woodsmen all, when caught alone by nightfall in the woods, shelter themselves in a little one-man bark covering that looks for all the world like the grave houses used by these Redmen before the days of lumber; in fact, were a little pole erected in front with a white rag hanging at the top, a traveler chancing along would surely think that the mortal remains of some poor soul who is now with his fathers was resting there beneath the sod. Today these little grave houses are made of lumber instead of bark.

But it's the shelter for the living that concerns us: Secure two straight green shoots of any kind of wood, sharpen the ends and thrust them in the ground to form two arches just high enough for one to crawl under, and spaced six feet apart, as in Figure 5. Connect these with three lengthwise poles of very light stuff as shown, and tie to the arches. Then peel the bark from a cedar, spruce, or elm tree and lay over the top, tying the bark to the arches in a couple of places with thongs of elm or basswood bark.

Figure 5. INDIAN BARK KENNEL

The Indian would spread a few fir boughs on the ground, build a little fire at each end for a mosquito smudge, and crawl in; or if no mosquitoes, he might use only one fire and close the foot end with an upright slab of bark.

For full instruction on stripping bark in large sheets for such purposes as this, see page 43.

TENTS FOR THE TRAIL

The perfect tent for all purposes does not exist. An ideal tent in one situation might be an abomination in another. What do we look for in a tent? First, *shelter from rain;* second, *protection from mosquitoes* and other *insect pests;* third, *warmth.* And withal the tent must be light in weight and compact in volume—easy to haul and to pack.

None of these points can be neglected in selecting a shelter. Any tent will give protection from rain—one type is about as good as another if that is all that is desired. But a tent designed to keep out mosquitoes, flies and no-see-ums will be damp and cold as a morgue on a chilly night, because cold nights require an open tent into which the heat of the fire can be reflected—it's a curious fact that the colder the weather the more open the tent must be. To camp with an open tent on a summer night will mean that you will be eaten alive by mosquitoes, and to camp on a cold night with an enclosed tent will mean hours of shivering and the unpleasantness of being confined in a damp, dismal and cheerless hovel. In short, summer camping requires one type of tent, cold nights another type—and so if one is to be equipped with shelter for all emergencies, he must have two tents. Which to take depends on when and where you are going.

No one familiar with the trails and portages will lightly brush aside the question of weight—there is enough to haul without the added grief of a bulky and bundlesome tent. A good-sized man cannot pack more than fifty to sixty pounds for longer than an hour without making a pack-horse out of himself, and robbing himself of the joy of the trip. No adolescent boy should haul more than twenty-five pounds for any length of time and ten pounds is considered right for girls. Consequently, careful attention should be given to the weight and bulkiness of the material from which the tent is made.

Let us consider the tent materials first, then the acceptable styles for warm weather and for cold weather.

LIGHT-WEIGHT TENT MATERIALS

The standard duck from which ordinary wall and similar large tents are made is much too heavy and cumbersome for the compact shelters demanded for canoe cruising and general wilderness use. Such canvas has long since been out-moded and replaced with "featherweight" materials by canoeists, explorers and sportsmen who know the trail.

There are several excellent cloths available which are remarkably light in weight, absolutely waterproof, sturdy and tough enough for years of the hardest use, and so thin that the tent will roll into a surprisingly small bundle. Any of these will make a stronger, lighter, more enduring, and more waterproof tent than will duck or canvas.

The more popular and widely used of these light-weight tent materials are *tanalite*, *Egyptian cloth*, *aberlite*, *kiro*, *tano*, *"extra light,"* and *balloon silk*.

Egyptian cloth is an excellent tent material but a trifle heavier than the others and so is not used in making the lightest and smallest tents. Tanalite is probably the best of all materials for light-weight tents, its remarkable strength making possible an unusually thin cloth and producing a tent that will wear for a lifetime. The so-called "extra light" material is practically of the same standard of excellence. Aberlite makes a very good tent, slightly heavier but cheaper in price— of the medium priced materials it is to be preferred. For an indication of the relative weights of the five most widely used of these cloths, a tent weighing seven pounds in tanalite would also weigh about seven pounds in "extra light," 7¼ pounds in aberlite, 7½ pounds in kiro, and 8¾ pounds in Egyptian.

A tent made of any of these cloths will be a joy forever. It will call for more of an expenditure than a canvas or duck tent but the satisfaction, convenience and comfort one will obtain from it throughout long years of service will make it a cheap investment after all.

Light-weight ponchos or ground cloths are best made of *alligator cloth*, either in standard light-weight or in featherweight. Rubber ponchos or sheets are much too heavy to be considered.

TENTS FOR WARM WEATHER

A tent for summer camping must be rainproof and vermin-proof —particularly the latter for one can put up with a little leakage and spray in his face, if necessary, better than with the hordes of mosquitoes, flies, gnats, no-see-ums and the scores of other pests without end that infest the woods in the summer. No experienced person would tackle the woods during fly and mosquito season without all possible protection. In other words, the tent must have a ground-cloth and insect-proof coverings for all openings.

The type of tent one would take on the trail in the summer would depend upon how many people are in the party, but the best plan is to select tents suitable in size for two people, which in a pinch will accommodate three, and if there are more in the party, to take additional tents of the same size. A tent of this size brings to mind something on the order of a pup-tent but the ordinary old style pup-tent invariably proves to be a false friend, failing us when its protection is most needed. Wide open at one end, and often at both ends, it offers a constant invitation to the hordes of mosquitoes to come in and partake generously of a buffet supper. Without a ground-cloth it offers no protection below and the open ends give little defense against rain. Such pup-tents are out of the question as acceptable equipment for one going into the woods on a trip of some length, and to send campers out from summer camps on trips with them seems like a deliberate scheme to prevent their happiness and enjoyment of the expedition. No camper should be asked to sleep in the woods without mosquito protection, and no tent is acceptable unless it provides such protection one-hundred per cent. Furthermore, no tent is worth hauling along unless it erects a barrier to moisture in all directions—below, above, sidewards, backwards, and frontwards— and that no matter what turn the weather takes. What type of tent will meet these conditions?

Let us consider the matter first from the standpoint of the person who wishes a first-class tent for woods travel and who is willing to buy the best because he knows it will last a lifetime barring accidents, and secondly, from the standpoint of the boys and girls and others who want an adequate protection at a reasonable cost.

The Explorer's Tent.—In Figure 6 we have the most popular design for light woodland travel. It has a sewed-in ground-cloth and a bobbinet door with zipper opening, making it absolutely pest-proof. There is a screened and hooded ventilator in the roof. It can be set up with an inside pole placed in the middle of the door, with ropes tied to trees as in the drawing, or with scissor poles outside as illustrated.

This style of tent can be obtained in a variety of sizes. The so-called *One Man Tent* is the tiniest and lightest tent made, 4½ by 6½ feet long, and is, as the name implies, suitable for one person only. The *Ideal Cruiser Tent* is the same tent but larger, suitable for two campers, measuring five by seven feet—this is the tent preferred for canoe trips. Then comes the *Explorer's Tent* proper which is more spacious, varying from 7½ by 7¼ feet, to 9½ by 7¼ feet.

The Ideal Cruiser Tent made of tanalite or other cloth of equal weight is the perfect shelter for two men on a canoe trip or other expedition in the summer, rainproof, vermin-proof, and "light as a feather." It will be found wanting for summer travel only on one score: the sewed-in ground-cloth accumulates dirt no end—boots will bring in mud, and with the circular or rectangular doors elevated as they are a few inches from the ground, there is no chance to sweep or shake the dirt out other than by the dustpan method. Furthermore, hobnails are hard on sewed-in ground-cloths, and for safety's sake, lanterns must give way to flashlights on them. To facilitate cleaning, some campers prefer a tent without the ground-cloth sewed in but with a six-inch ground flap or sod-cloth all around, and a separate ground-cloth which can be laid over the ground when desired. These objections to the use of sewed-in ground-cloths become serious in a large tent in a permanent camp but not particularly so in these pocket-sized shelters—such tents are used only as shifting camps and

Figure 6. EXPLORER'S TENT FOR SUMMER

they do not remain in place long enough to accumulate much dirt, and being small there is no walking on the ground-cloth with hobnails.

Tents of the Explorer's pattern are designed to conserve all possible material. They slope down at the foot where height serves no purpose, but are high at the front, the Explorer's Tent proper being high enough for one to stand and the Cruiser model high enough to kneel while dressing. It should be remembered that these tents are sleeping shelters only and are not designed to give room to walk about.

There are many styles of tents on this general order, such as the *Canoe Tent*, the *Compac Tent*, the *George Tent*, the *Hudson Bay Tent*, and the *Ross Alpine Tent*, all well known and obtainable from first-class camp outfitters and each with its good points. Between these various models the choice is one of personal preference, but it is probably true that the Explorer's model is the outgrowth of experimentation with these other and older types and has a greater following among trail experts than any of these. The *Miner's Tent*, a time-honored model, is a small pyramidal tent but offers no insect protection and therefore is less often used by those campers who frequent the lake and woods country.

Insect-Proof Pup-Tent.—Unfortunately the tents of the Explorer's type made of the very light-weight material are out of range in price for the average boy and girl, and especially for use as issued or required equipment for trips in organized camps. And as already indicated, the old-style pup-tent or shelter-half, lacking as it does the absolutely essential requisite of insect protection, does not merit consideration. There is an over-tent of mosquito netting made for the pup-tent, sometimes used in the army, but this is a nuisance and not to be recommended except possibly for tropical use.

However, wedge tents of the size and shape of the traditional pup-tent are available with ground-cloth sewed in, with the back closed, and with a sewed-in front of mosquito netting equipped with a zipper. These cost but a little more than the ordinary pup-tents and offer all of the advantages of protection from insects and ground dampness. Made of canvas they are of course heavy and bulky as compared to the lighter materials, but for the type of use to which boys and girls usually put them, and for the needs of the organized camp, this is not such an important matter. The shape of the wedge tent is not so convenient as that of the Explorer's model because of the lack of head room, but something must be sacrificed for simplicity and the resultant saving in the time and cost of making. There are some sportsmen who prefer the shape of the wedge tent, however, feeling that the Explorer's type is a little fussy, and for such campers the wedge type can be obtained in one of the light-weight materials.

Woodcraft means nothing if not living comfortably in the woods. The idea that a good camper should "take it" without complaint, which has often led to the sending of children into the woods without adequate protection, can find no common-sense justification. So often has a potentially glorious trip into the woods terminated in a nightmare of distress because of insect pests that the open pup-tent and its like have become taboo—good vermin-proof ones are too inexpensive and easy to obtain.

TENTS FOR COLD NIGHTS

Cold, wet, and dismal indeed is the little pocket-sized tent of the Explorer's type on a rainy or chilly night. Seated by the warmth and glow of the friendly fire, one hates to think of bedtime approaching because it means departure to the cold, uninviting tent. Fire is precious in the woods—if not for heat, its dancing flames mean friendliness and cheer and hominess. The closed tent is dark and drab and inhospitable—but one must often sacrifice the sight of the fire in summer for the freedom from insects that the closed tent offers. When nights are cold, however, the mosquito hordes no longer menace and the warmth of fire becomes the prime concern. And so the enclosed tent must give way to the open-sided one that gives free access to the campfire. Hence one needs two tents to meet the exigencies and contingencies of camping in all seasons of the year—a summer tent and one for colder weather.

An open-sided canvas *lean-to*, with one side entirely exposed to the weather is the type that gives promise of warmth and cheer in cold weather, for a roaring reflector fire may be built in front, radiating its warmth and healthful rays within. The Baker Tent is such a shelter, long popular in the timber country. From the picture of it in Figure 7 it will be noted that there is ample headroom, an awning extension out in front, and a sloping shed roof. When a fire is built in front the angle of the roof reflects and throws down the heat on much the same principle as is made use of in a reflecting baker, drying the ground and keeping the blankets warm throughout the night. This tent is really half of a wall tent.

The front extension constitutes a door which may be dropped and tied shut when you are away from the tent, and a sunshade when tied up as an awning during the daytime. The awning is usually left tied out in front if the night is warm enough so that no fire is needed, but on cold nights it is thrown back over the roof of the tent and out of the way so as not to interfere with the fire. For the best results the reflector fire should be placed six feet in front of the opening of the tent.

This type of tent may be put up by means of a rope tied to trees as in Figure 7, or with poles arranged as shears at each end.

Baker Tents can be made in any of the light-weight tent materials. One with a seven-foot front in tanalite will weigh slightly over seven pounds.

Figure 7. BAKER TENT FOR COLD WEATHER

Campfire Tent.—The best style of Baker Tent is the variation shown in B, Figure 7, called the Campfire Tent. It will be noticed that the ridge is moved back, thus giving greater height and head-room, and producing a steeper roof which sheds rain and snow much better, yet at the same time sacrificing nothing in its capacity to reflect the heat of the fire.

Tarpaulin Tent.—A large sheet of canvas 10 by 14 feet in size may be arranged so as to produce three tents in one and at the same time serve a number of other needs in camp. It may be set up as a lean-to serving the same purpose as the Baker Tent, as shown in A, Figure 8 —if the ends are banked with boughs this will make a good enough cold-weather shelter but needless to say should not be classed with the Baker or Campfire Tent. Or, if tapes are sewed along the lines of the pattern to serve as reinforcements, and grommets are sewed in at the points indicated, it may be set up as a modified Miner's Tent with a perpendicular front as in B, Figure 8. Again it may be set up as a wedge tent by merely hanging it over a horizontal rope and pegging down the corners as in C. Then, too, it may be pressed into service as a ground-cloth and will also do duty as a wrapping for the outfit.

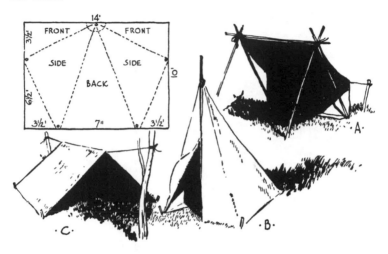

Figure 8. TARPAULIN TENT

Lean-to Tent.—A plain piece of sheeting 7 by 9 feet in size, if set up at an angle of forty-five degrees, will make a reflecting roof for a night that is not too cold. The ends should be banked with boughs if the weather is bad.

Forester's Tent.—Here is a cold-weather tent of a different shape, somewhat on the order of the Explorer's Tent but with a wide-open front so designed as to catch the heat of the fire in front. Figure 9 shows it. It is a good and efficient tent, cozy and warm in the worst of weather.

WATERPROOFING AND DYEING

All tents of light-weight materials and most canvas or duck tents are thoroughly waterproofed when purchased. If one wishes to obtain the cloth and make his own tent, however, thorough waterproofing will be necessary, particularly if canvas is used. There are several ready-prepared waterproofing mixtures which can be purchased for the purpose, information regarding which can be obtained from any of the larger camp-outfitting companies.

It is very easy to prepare the solutions for waterproofing ourselves, however, but before this is undertaken a choice must be made between the chemical process relying on the use of alum and the paraffin proc-

Figure 9. FORESTER'S TENT

ess. There are points in favor of each: The chemical, or alum process will coat the threads of the fabric so that the tent will shed water effectively provided the roof has enough slope so that it can run off, but if puddles are permitted to gather on the cloth there will be some seepage. This process adds nothing to the weight or pliability of the cloth and in no way changes its appearance. The cloth becomes practically immune to mildew and, if anything, is made stronger and more enduring. The cloth may be treated either before or after it is made up into the tent.

The paraffin method is designed to coat the surface of the fabric so as to make it completely watertight. However, when so treated the canvas takes on increased weight and becomes less flexible. A further disadvantage rests in the fact that the paraffined canvas does not permit air to pass through it.

The Alum Method.—There are two well-known mixtures based upon alum, one combining it with sugar-of-lead and the other with laundry soap.

The alum-and-sugar-of-lead treatment is as follows: Dissolve alum in hot water using one-fourth pound to each gallon, making enough of the solution to cover the fabric. In another container dissolve sugar-of-lead in hot water using one-fourth pound to the gallon. Soak the canvas in the alum mixture and allow it to remain for several hours, or overnight if you desire. Then wring it out and submerge it in the sugar-of-lead solution for an equal length of time. When wrung out and dried the tent will be ready to use.

Two important points to remember: First, sugar-of-lead is a poison. Second, the water used must be soft water or rain water, free from lime.

For the alum-and-soap process, shave up ordinary laundry soap and dissolve it in hot water in the proportion of one large bar to the gallon, stirring until it is thoroughly dissolved. The alum mixture is prepared just as for the alum-and-sugar-of-lead treatment. Soak the cloth first in the soap solution, then hang it up and let it drip dry. Then soak in the alum solution as before.

Paraffin Method.—There are two methods of applying paraffin— the rubbing method and the soaking method:

For the rubbing method, first iron the tent so as to remove all wrinkles, then rub it with a block of paraffin until it is thoroughly coated to the extent that it shows the white of the paraffin. Now iron it again with a warm iron—for this purpose it is well to use an old-fashioned (non-electric) iron because it is important that too much heat be avoided. The heat sets the paraffin and the canvas becomes waterproof.

For the soaking method, enough turpentine is needed to cover the cloth. Into this put shaved paraffin in the proportion of about one pound to the gallon. Heat this mixture by placing the container in a larger vessel containing very hot water and stir until the paraffin is dissolved. Now erect the tent and paint the canvas with the hot mixture using a large brush and working very rapidly because the mixture must not be permitted to get cold. *Turpentine is inflammable and therefore this method is dangerous.* Better avoid it—the other methods will serve the purpose and are safe.

Dyeing.—The glare of a white tent is hard on the eyes and causes it to stand out much too conspicuously when viewed against the green background of the forest. Very few of the better tents of the light-weight type are made of white materials. Colored cloth—green or brown—is restful to the eyes, blends delightfully with the woods setting, is inconspicuous, and does not attract flies like white tents do. Canvas and other tent materials may be dyed with ordinary cloth dyes just as any other type of cotton cloth is treated.

CHAPTER II

TEPEES OF THE PLAINS

THE MOST beautiful and colorful movable home in all the world is the tepee of the plains. And it is the nearest to the ideal canvas dwelling that has ever been devised, for a little fire within makes it cozy and warm in winter, the smoke-flaps provide perfect ventilation, the sides roll up to offer a breezy, cool and shady place in summer, and the wide base provides a foundation that is impregnable in any gale short of a cyclone. But more important still is its romantic appeal—it is full of memories, rich in imagination—its voice speaks a poetic language that all youth understands.

With its obvious superiorities one wonders why it is so seldom used. The reason rests in its one serious shortcoming—it requires about twenty long poles which must either be hauled along or cut each time the tepee is erected, and that is such a formidable and time-consuming task as to taboo the tepee as a shelter for a moving camp. General George C. Sibley, an old Indian fighter, was so impressed with the tepee as an unequaled shelter that he designed a tent on its general plan that required only one pole, this in the center, a tent which has been used with slight modifications in the army ever since and carries the name of the Sibley Tent, but the one pole is also very heavy and its presence in the center destroys the salient advantage of the tepee, that of building an open campfire within. It is when we are staying put at one camp for some time that the tepee comes into its own as a uniquely satisfying lodge.

Every organized camp should possess tepees—if not for use as sleeping quarters, two or three should be had for decoration, for so completely and compellingly do they symbolize the spirit of camping and so uniquely ornamental are they that no camp seems properly dressed without them. They will find many romantic uses and the making is a challenging project full of tradition and luster, well within the capacity of any wide-awake group of boys and girls.

It has been said that no one but an old Plains Indian squaw can handle a fire in a tepee so as to make the lodge resemble anything but a smoke house in full blast, but this is scarcely so. True, you must have sound, dry wood selected to burn and not to create a smoke smudge, and the fire must be small, for indeed a large one would roast you out in short order—I know of no shelter that heats up so thoroughly with so tiny a fire. Given a good little fire, the trick of smoke riddance rests in the manipulation of the smoke-flaps, a knack that will be mastered with a little practice so that the lower air can be kept clear with just enough smoke permeating the tent to warn the mosquitoes to stay out, and to provide that delightful perfume which has no equal to those who have traveled the far trails and dwelt in the silent places.

The word tepee comes from the Dakota word *tipi*—*ti* meaning "dwelling" and *pi* "used for," hence "used for a dwelling." But the Sioux *i* is pronounced as *e* in this word, thus the origin of the English spelling, *tepee.*

The tepee is a contribution of the Plains Indians. In fact, so characteristic is it of them that it and the eagle-feather headdress have come to symbolize these riders of the prairies and hunters of the buffalo. We find it across the wide frontier of prairie-land, used alike by the Dakota, the Assiniboin, the Blackfoot, the Cheyenne, the Arapaho, the Missouri, the Omaha, and the Crow, among others. In its present form and size, however, it is a relatively recent development. In the old days the Sioux and most neighboring tribes dwelt in lodges made of sod and poles, partly underground. These were octagonal in shape, perhaps twenty feet across, the lower half underground and the roof a few feet above the level of the earth, covered with solidly packed dirt. There were two entrances, one a sloping runway that led down from ground level, and the other a hole in the middle of the roof which admitted light, served for ventilation, allowed the smoke of the open fire under it to escape, and by means of a ladder connecting it with the floor, served as an emergency entrance and exit as well as a lookout for enemies. It was the presence of this smoke hole in the roof that meant the undoing of the Sioux in northern Wisconsin and Minnesota, where once they vied with the Chippewa for these hunting grounds, for the Chippewa, long friendly with the white men, secured gunpowder before the Sioux did, and by creeping up on the earth roof of their enemy's hut were able to drop powder into the fire beneath, causing an explosion that killed all within. Thus the Sioux were forced to migrate farther to the westward.

Now these earth-and-sod underground dwellings were the year-around or base homes of the Plains Redmen but being immovable, they did not serve fully the needs of a roving, buffalo-hunting people —hence the development of the tepee for the summer days of wandering and the long hunting treks. That was the purpose for which the tepee was developed and the use to which it was confined. Nor would it have served well as a permanent shelter because the tepees of these early days were very small—ten to twelve feet measured up the sloping walls. Why so small? Because the poles had to be dragged from place to place by dogs, since horses were still unknown on the plains, and of necessity had to be very slender, so much so that they bent under the weight of the hide covering, giving the tepee walls a sagged appearance.

Came the horse as a Godsend to these people, and the tepee overnight bloomed forth full grown. Sixteen to twenty feet in typical height, some up to twenty-five feet, they became of ample size for the family dwelling, and with surprising suddenness the sod-and-pole huts of the Sioux were relegated to the seven thousand years of yesterday. Tepees of stunning picturesqueness sprang up across the plains like mushrooms in a bumper season and became the prairie's most colorful man-made characteristic throughout the last century until, sadly, the white avalanche began to sweep them aside and herd the proud Redmen into despicable log and board hovels.

It was from the younger spring-killed buffalo that the hides were taken, for at that season the hair began to shed and the hides were thinner. Only for one year did a tepee give service, for even though in apparently good condition, the rigors of use would jeopardize the family's comfort before a second season was over, and so each spring new tepees were made preparatory to the forthcoming hunts, all to be finished before the sun dance in June. A gala event was tepee-making day for, like the pioneer quilting party, the neighboring women gathered to feast, sew—and gossip. The most experienced cut the hides to shape and the others united them into the half-circle of the lodge.

Pure white were the newly made tepees, setting forth brilliantly their painted designs, but time soon turned their walls to brown and smoke smudged the tops to black. But while age robbed them of some of their daytime splendor, it added a brilliance to the night view, for old tepees became semi-transparent so as to render them luminous from the fire within against the blackness of the night. A glorious sight were these huge lustrous cones of the prairie nights long past,

Figure 10. THE TYPICAL TEPEE (Blackfoot)

even as are the canvas tepees with dancing flames within on a modern night.

The buffalo gone, the canvas of the white man became the shelter of Plains Redmen and a happy transition it was from a practical point of view, for the task of making was simplified and shortened, and the finished tepee lighter to haul and erect, more resistant to rain, and more quickly dried out.

Whether the young-sized tepees of the pre-horse days or the full grown ones of the later period, the lodges of the moving Sioux village were always arranged in a circle-within-a-circle—an outer circle of tepees inside of which was a second circle (and sometimes a third and fourth if the gathering of bands was large), all surrounding an open campus in the center of which stood the council tepee, and sometimes the chiefs' living tepees. Wood being scarce for pegs, a circle of stones was often placed around the bottom of the tepee, resting on the bottom flaps of the walls to hold it secure, and merely to be rolled aside when camp was broken. Even today circles of stones marking the outlines of the tepees of the old buffalo-hunting villages can be seen upon the plains, and with careful study it can be noticed that these little circles of rocks form themselves into a circle-within-a-circle, the inevitable layout of the plains villages of yester-year. Every band had its assigned position in the pattern of the village, and every family its place in its band area, so that if the hunter should come into the village at night, even though it had moved since he left home, he could go right to his lodge.

The council tepee in the center was sometimes huge in size, it being recorded by Maximilian that the tepee of Iron Shirt, the Blackfoot Chief, visited by him in 1833, approximated fifty feet in diameter.*

But regardless of where in the circle the tepee was located, *it was always erected so that it faced the east.* This was and is a hard and fast rule, no matter what the topography of the spot selected, or the direction of the wind at the moment.

The tepee is its own glory to those who know the Grass Wind of the ranges—it needs no apostles to exalt it. Its medicine is magic to all who are rooted in the earth, but it remained for Ernest Thompson Seton first to introduce it popularly some many years ago to the city-wise who of all folk need its spirit tonic. We may not need its shelter today, but it is wine to the imagination now as in the old Red days, and the spirit of youth demands it.

And so we must build one. But how? Let us see:

MAKING THE TEPEE

An undersized tepee is not to be recommended other than as a play tent for smaller children because its limited space makes it of scant practical value and it requires an artist to manipulate a fire in one successfully. Sixteen feet is the standard size and the one we shall describe—if smaller sizes are desired the diameter of the pattern may be easily cut down.

Fifty-four yards of ten-ounce duck will be required. Perhaps some old tarpaulins can be found to save the cost of new materials but be

---

* Maximilian, Prince of Wied. *Travels in the Interior of North America*, p. 261, London, 1843.

sure the canvas is unrotted for there is no point in putting all the work into a tepee that will soon rip.

In addition, the following materials are needed: six dozen half-inch iron grommets, large ball of strong string, sixty feet quarter-inch cotton rope, beeswax, sailor's needle and palm.

Cut the canvas in five lengths, thirty-three feet, thirty-two feet, twenty-nine feet, twenty-six feet and twenty feet. Mark the center

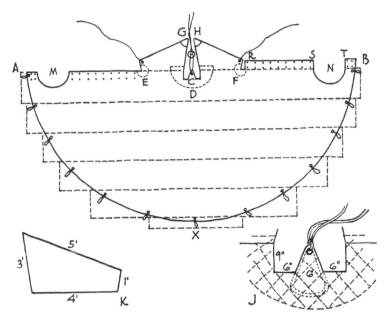

Figure 11. PATTERN FOR THE TEPEE OF THE PLAINS

of each to serve as a guide in sewing, and then machine-sew the strips together as indicated by the pattern in Figure 11, overlapping the edges in a one-inch seam and using a double row of stitches. A small piece of canvas a foot wide and six feet long must be sewed to the middle of one of the edges as indicated at X. Spread the canvas on the floor, stretch smoothly and tack the corners. Now drive a nail in the floor at O, which point is eighteen inches from the edge of the canvas at its exact middle, attach a strong string exactly sixteen feet long to this nail, at the end of which is a pencil, and mark the curved edge of the tepee. Trim off the canvas four inches from this line, the extra four inches providing a wide reinforcing hem when doubled under and sewed.

Now we must cut out the canvas to make the tie-flap at C, the pattern of which is blown up to a larger scale in the insert at J. Note that the cuts are to a depth of nine inches, that each notch is six inches wide, and the tie-flap itself is six inches wide at the base and nine inches long, shaped as shown. This tie-flap is subjected to great strain, in fact it must hold up the entire weight of the tepee, and so the canvas must be reinforced by a second piece sewed underneath and quilted with crosswise stitching as indicated by the dotted lines. If the tepee rips at this point its days of usefulness are over, and so as an additional precaution it is well to insert a loop of rope between the two layers of canvas before the quilting is done, as indicated in J, which will prevent the strain from becoming localized too much at the tip. Sew a grommet at the extreme tip as shown, through which a two-foot rope is tied at its middle.

Now cut the two smoke-flaps according to the pattern shown in K, and sew in place as indicated in the large pattern. At E and at F a reinforcing piece of canvas must be sewed on the underside as indicated by the dotted lines. At the tip of each smoke flap, G and H, a pocket about four inches deep is made by sewing on a triangular piece of canvas, into which the end of the smoke-flap pole is inserted to hold the flap in position, as illustrated in A, Figure 14. An alternative method is to make a hole at the tip about three inches wide through which the pole is thrust as in B, Figure 14.

Next cut the door holes, M and N, each three feet wide and semi-circular. Tepee doors vary greatly in shape, but the circular opening makes an attractive front. The edges should be turned to make a one-inch hem.

Now the strip of canvas R S must be sewed in place which is eight inches wide and extends from the bottom of the smoke-flap to the door, overlapped one inch in sewing thus leaving a seven-inch extension. A piece of equal width is sewed below the door at T B. Note that these extensions are only on one side of the tepee. Now the double row of grommets must be installed between A and E for the lacing pins by means of which the tepee is laced shut when erected. The outer holes are one inch from the edge, the two holes of each pair are five inches from each other and the pairs spaced nine inches apart. The corresponding holes in the extension on the other side, between R and B, must now be cut, measured so as to exactly match those between A and E. A grommet is sewed in each of these holes. A grommet is also placed at the lower corner of each smoke-flap and a twenty-foot rope tied to each. Grommets should also be sewed every two feet around the curved edge, through which short loops of rope are tied to serve as tent-peg loops.

The canvas is now ready for decoration.

Should a tepee smaller than sixteen feet be desired it is well to cut the canvas into an exact half-circle. Such a plan has been successfully followed for many years by Ernest Thompson Seton in constructing twelve-foot tepees for use in camps and Indian villages.*

ERECTING THE TEPEE

Eighteen to twenty poles are needed for the frame of the tepee and for the sake of a neat, well-dressed lodge it pays to go to great pains in selecting smooth, straight ones. A first-class set of poles was a costly item on the plains, frequently considered as of greater value than the tepee itself, for the prairie was a scanty provider when it came to wood, and long trips to the mountains or woodlands were necessary to secure them. Lodgepole pine, cedar and spruce were the preferred woods of the Plains Indians. The bark was peeled and the poles scraped until the wood of the outer ring, that of the last year's growth, had been removed. A squaw was proud of her tepee poles and looked upon them as the badge of good housekeeping.

The poles should be about twenty feet long for a sixteen-foot tepee, two-and-one-half inches thick at the butt and one inch at the top. Having secured the straightest ones the thicket will produce, regardless of the kind of wood, peel and smooth them up with a drawknife. At best the poles will be none too straight if saplings are cut for the purpose. If in the city the best plan is to have them cut from milled lumber, two inches square and uniform in length, and then to round off the edges with a drawknife. Another city possibility is found in large bamboo poles.

There are two well-known methods of erecting the poles, the more

---

* See Ernest Thompson Seton, *The Book of Woodcraft*, page 468 (Garden City, Garden City Publishing Co., 1921); also Julia M. Buttree, *Rhythm of the Redman*, p. 233 (New York: A. S. Barnes and Co., 1930).

commonly used one being the setting up of a tripod of three poles as a foundation. Select the three best poles for this and lay aside a fourth good one for the lifting pole. Spread the canvas on the ground and lay two poles side by side directly up the middle of the canvas, extending six inches below the curved edge and lying directly across the tie-flap. Now lay the third pole along one of the straight edges of the tepee so that it crosses the two poles at right angles. Tie the three poles together with the end of a twenty-foot rope as shown in A, Figure 12, and set up the tripod, allowing the long end of the rope to hang down in the center. The third pole, the single one in A, is the door pole and is placed at X in C, Figure 12, so that it will be on the left as one enters. A tripod tied in this way must be so spread

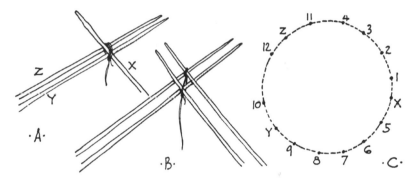

Figure 12. ARRANGEMENT OF POLES IN ERECTING THE TEPEE

that it will lock—this will be achieved if the poles x, y, and z in A are placed so that they are in the positions of x, y, and z in C. The other poles may now be laid on the tripod in the order shown in C. It will be noted that there is a pole missing in the vacant space directly opposite the door—this is for the lifting pole which will be placed when the canvas is hoisted.

The other method of setting up the frame consists in using four poles tied together as in B, instead of the tripod, which when spread form a square, the door being midway of one of the sides of the square. The poles are then laid in first on the two sides of the tepee, next on the back side, and lastly the front, the last two poles being the door poles.

Spread the poles so that the circle formed by the butts is a little less than the circumference of the tepee. Now anchor the frame by wrapping the rope around the poles at the intersection a couple of

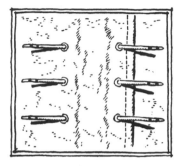

times and then tying the end to a peg driven in the ground near the center of the lodge. If the lodge is only to stand for a short time this anchor peg may be eliminated and the rope tied down along one of the poles.

Figure 13. METHOD OF LAC-
ING THE FRONT OF THE TEPEE
WITH STICKS

Now to hoist the canvas: Lay the lifting pole across the middle of the cover as it is spread on the ground, the butt extending as usual six inches below the curved edge and the top resting across the tie-flap. Tie the tie-flap securely to it, fold the canvas over the pole, and lift all into position, the pole being placed in the space left vacant opposite the door. Then spread the canvas around the tepee and it is ready to be laced in front. Twelve slender sticks are needed for the

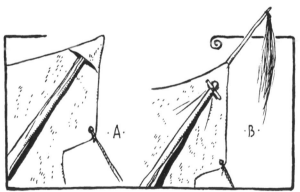

Figure 14. TWO METHODS OF INSERTING THE POLES IN THE SMOKE-FLAPS

lacing, fifteen inches long and of the thickness of a pencil. Beginning at the top, run the sticks through the holes as indicated in Figure 13.

Finish the job by spreading the poles and driving the tent pegs, but the spreading should be done carefully and gradually, else the tepee will "walk" out of position. The two smoke-flap poles should be slender and light, and are poked into the pocket as in A, Figure 14, or through the hole in the smoke-flap as in B. If the latter plan is used a short cross-stick should be tied across the pole near the end to form a shoulder to prevent slipping, as seen in B. A strand from a horse's tail will give the pole a typical Plains appearance.

The fireplace is a little to the back of center, and consists of a slight excavation 12 to 15 inches in diameter with edges lined with stones. *The fire must be very small* both for safety and comfort, for the sloping walls reflect the heat so effectively that it does not take much of a blaze to turn the place into a bake oven. To draw out the smoke the smoke-flaps should be so arranged that the opening is *away from the wind.* When there is no wind the flaps are turned back opening the top widely. In case the wind is from the east the flaps are closed and the door left open, thus causing a draft that lifts the smoke to the center opening above. In case of rain the flaps are shut completely.

Figure 15. TEPEE DOORS

The tepee door consists of a piece of canvas cut to shape and edged with an open hem through which flexible branches are inserted as shown in Figure 15. The door should overlap the opening at least six inches all around, and so in the pattern we are using which has a three-foot opening, the door should be four feet in diameter. Doors vary greatly in shape, some being circular or oblong as in A, and some with a straight bottom as in B. A loop is attached to the top which is hung over one of the lacing pins.

Remember that the tepee is always set up so as to face the east—the time-honored tradition of the plains permits no liberties here.

The Dew-Cloth

The inner wall of an authentic Plains Indian tepee has a lining of canvas extending up from the ground a few feet. This is called a dew-cloth and is a most ingenious device that not only adds a colorful touch to the interior but has great practical value in eliminating direct drafts from under the walls of the tepee, throwing the incoming air upward and sending it on its way to the smoke-flaps above, clearing the smoke out with it. A further service that the dew-cloth renders is to catch the water which runs down the poles in a heavy rain, thus preventing it from dripping onto the beds.

A diagram of the dew-cloth is shown in Figure 16 and the interiors of two Blackfoot tepees with dew-cloths in place are shown in Figures 20 and 21. The interior in Figure 21 is interesting in that it not only shows the placement of the dew-cloth and its design, but also a Blackfoot stick bed, several decorated parfleche bags leaning against the walls, and several headdress carriers hanging from the poles. The fireplace excavation can also be seen, in front of which is the anchor stake and anchor rope holding the tepee secure.

Figure 16. THE DEW-CLOTH— THE INTERIOR LINING OF THE TEPEE

Dew-cloths vary from four to six feet in height, but the most convenient size for our purpose is six feet, made by sewing together two three-foot strips of lightweight canvas. Grommets should be sewed along the lower edge, spaced a foot apart with rope loops attached so that the bottom of the dew-cloth may be pegged down very close to the ground. Additional grommets should be placed along the top edge with which to tie the cloth to the tepee poles.

These dew-cloths are always ornamented with painted designs of which those appearing in Figure 16 and in the photographs, Figures 20 and 21, are typical.

Figure 17. A BLACKFOOT TEPEE   *Figure 18.* A BLACKFOOT TEPEE

Figure 19. BLACKFOOT TEPEES

DECORATING THE TEPEE

Far more important than any physical needs the tepee may serve is its ministry to the spirit—its imaginative glow, its poetry. And this ministry is given eloquence and fullness of meaning by the parables of line and color in the Indian's true symbolic fashion ornamenting its up-sweeping walls. Add the blaze of color, the arresting design, that the tepee may fill its mission truly.

But unless handled discreetly a paint brush may well undo an otherwise good tepee, for the mere fact that by tradition it is an Indian lodge places certain limitations on design. Unless one is thoroughly conversant with Indian conventions he will do better to copy accurately a lodge well decorated by the hand of an Indian than to attempt to improvise and improve.

The more typical tepees of the plains usually show a border around the bottom and a colored point at the top, often with additional symbols such as animals or hoof prints on the walls. Characteristic Blackfoot designs are in Figures 17, 18, 19 and 22. It will be noted that these Indians are much given to the use of round spots both in the bottom border and on the painted top—these symbolize stars, while the triangular or semicircular border tops shown in the Blackfoot borders in Figure 22 represent mountains. In drawing the animals on the walls it is particularly important that Indian originals be copied literally for these are not true-to-life pictures but conventionalized ones—note the line in the body, the life line that all such animal symbols possess.

Often the personal symbol of the owner of the lodge is seen on the tepee. This is usually placed in the middle of the back side at the top, directly behind the smoke-flaps.

Some Plains Indian tepees show certain episodes in the life histories of their owners. While intriguing from the Indian standpoint, such figures do not make particularly striking decorations for our purpose. The bold designs of the type shown in the accompanying illustrations are more suitable.

The layout of a Blackfoot tepee spread flat is shown in Figure 23. From this pattern the method of applying any of the designs shown in the illustrations can be understood. First spread out the tepee smoothly on the floor, then tie a piece of chalk or crayon to a string attached to a nail and mark all semicircular lines. The round spots

Figure 20. INTERIOR OF A BLACKFOOT TEPEE SHOWING DEW-CLOTH

Figure 21. A BLACKFOOT TEPEE INTERIOR SHOWING DEW-CLOTH, WIL-
LOW BED, AND PARFLECHE BAGS

Figure 22. BLACKFOOT TEPEES SHOWING TYPICAL DECORATIONS

are best applied by cutting out a circle of cardboard and tracing around it.

The two predominant colors should be ultramarine blue and Chinese red, with chrome yellow, black, and white used more sparingly. No color stands out so vividly or carries so far in the woods as does blue. The round spots on the Blackfoot tepees are very effective in white against a solid background of blue or red. While some tepees are painted all over, it is better to rely on the natural color of the canvas for the general background and to paint only the designs—the unpainted canvas will be lighter in weight, more pliable, and more lasting. Use ordinary house paint, if good colors can be found, and thin it

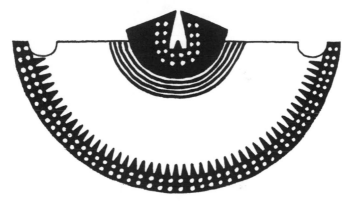

Figure 23. A Tepee Decoration, Spread Flat

with a little Japan dryer. If you will wet the canvas with water before painting, the colored areas will not be so stiff nor so inclined to crack after the paint dries. Large brushes will be needed for the solid areas and narrow lining brushes for the finishing and touching.

Hair from a horse's tail very frequently adds effective ornamentation to a tepee, particularly on the smoke-flaps. A tuft may be hung from each of the lower corners of the flaps, or tufts tied at intervals up the front edge of the flaps. If the smoke-flaps are of the type that has a hole through which the pole is thrust, rather than a pocket, a streamer of hair should be attached to the top of each of the poles as seen in B, Figure 14.

Even as inconspicuous an item as the tent pegs were not neglected by the Indian in his desire to beautify his lodge. Slender, straight sticks were used, each with a band or two of color circling the top. So, too, the lacing sticks up the front were made vivid with colored stripes around them.

CHAPTER III

BARK WIGWAMS AND SHELTERS

To ASK what type of shelter the American Indian used is just about as futile a question as to inquire what style of dwelling is characteristic of the white man in America. There were as many types as there were cultured areas and sections of the country. As the natural environment varied from arctic wastes to woods, to plains, to mesas, the type of shelter varied, depending upon the materials the environment offered and the culture of the tribe.

The Plains Indians with little bark and an abundance of buffalo hide fashioned their tepees from hide, while their brothers of the woods with bark aplenty and little thick hide, used the bark. These bark shelters of the Woodland Indians, particularly of the Chippewas, have always fascinated me. No other type of lodge is so close to the earth, so at home in the world of growing things.

Wigwams most people seem to picture in their minds as being pointed or cone-shaped—the bark counterpart of the canvas or hide tepee—but this pointed style was far from the most characteristic and commonly used dwelling in the northern woodlands. Rather, the dome-shaped wigwam or *waginogan* (pronounced wä′ge-noo-gän′) was the permanent year-around shelter of the timber folk, the pointed bark type or *nasa-ogan* (pronounced nä′sa-o-gän′) being used only in the temporary camps during the summer months when the family was moving frequently from one place to another. The idea of "home" centered around the dome-shaped waginogan. In the old days such wigwams were the common dwellings of the many tribes from Canada to North Carolina, including the Chippewas, the Crees, the Sauk, the Foxes, the Iowas, the Winnebagos, the Menominees, and the Potawatomis.

The word *wigwam* does not properly apply to pointed or cone-shaped dwellings at all. While to the Chippewas, *wigwam*, or as they pronounce it, *wigiwam*, means any kind of a dwelling, or dwellings in general, long usage in English limits its meaning to the dome-shaped shelter or waginogan, while the word *tepee* covers all kinds of pointed or cone-shaped dwellings regardless of the material from which they are made, whether hide, canvas, or bark.

In addition to the dome-shaped waginogan and the pointed nasa-ogan, there are other types of bark shelters used by the Woodland Indians, particularly the bark houses with peaked roof and the bark lean-to. Each of these we shall discuss in detail.

THE DOME-SHAPED WIGWAM

Once one has had experience with a dome-shaped waginogan he will understand why the woods-wise Chippewa selected it over the other types of bark lodges as his permanent, year-around home. It is a compact, cozy, warm, convenient little lodge. And withal it is colorful—which aspect makes it an excellent addition to an organized camp where it will not only blend most acceptably and picturesquely with the camp setting but will provide a useful den, a romantic shelter for groups sleeping out, and a most appropriate headquarters for the woodcraft and the campcraft departments. Most camps have a few tepees arranged in an Indian village, or clustered around a council ring—such a layout most certainly should have a waginogan.

Building the Framework.—Select a picturesque spot in the woods for the wigwam and stake it out, marking on the ground the circle the walls are to follow. The lodge is slightly oblong in shape, a little longer than it is wide, a good size being ten feet in width and eleven-and-one-half to twelve feet in length.

A quantity of long slender poles varying from ten to sixteen feet are needed for the framework. *Ironwood* is preferred for these poles by the Indians when it can be obtained, it being very pliable when green and strong, durable and *elastic* when dry. Tamarack is often used with excellent results and *maple* sometimes employed when more durable woods with sufficient elasticity cannot be found. The poles should be as slender as can be found in the necessary lengths.

The frame we are to build with these slender poles is shown in A, Figure 24. First we must put in place the two poles that are to form the doorway of the waginogan—these are marked 1 and 2 in diagram B in Figure 24. The two longest and strongest poles should be selected for the doorway and placed two feet apart; sharpen the butts and force them into the ground six to ten inches, using a crowbar, if necessary, to make the holes. As these poles stand erect they should lean slightly to the outside, that is, away from the wigwam. Now put poles 3 and 4 in place in the same way, directly opposite 1 and 2 at the rear of the wigwam. Leaving these four poles standing straight up, install poles 5 and 6, and 7 and 8, each pair spaced two feet apart. Then proceed to put in place all the poles marked X in the diagram and all those marked Y. It will be noted that there are now eight poles on each of the long sides of the wigwam and six on each of the short sides, spaced uniformly. All these poles should lean outward a little as they stand erect.

Now bend poles 6 and 8 downward until they meet, forming an arch overhead about seven-and-one-half feet high. Tie them where they meet in the middle of the arch, then bend each end down along the opposite pole and tie to it. The traditional lashings for this purpose are well-soaked thongs of basswood bark, prepared according to the instructions given on page 210—no better lacings are obtainable than these. If "civilized" materials are to be used for tying, wire will make the most substantial wigwam.

Poles 5 and 7 should now be bent down in the same way, forming an arch of exactly the same height. Then proceed to bend down all the poles marked X, remembering that the arches must be progressively lower as we near the back and front of the wigwam since our purpose is to create the dome-shaped frame shown in A, Figure 24. The next task is to bend down the poles marked Y. Poles 1 and 3, and 2 and 4, are the last to be pulled down and tied. At each intersection of the crosswise and lengthwise poles, a lashing is placed.

The framework may now be completed by lashing on the horizontal poles—X, Y and Z in A, Figure 24. These may be of poplar if necessary since they are not particularly essential to the strength of the framework and are usually split in half to make them pliable enough to bend around the framework. The lower one, Z, is about four inches from the ground, while the upper one forms the top of the doorway and is usually about five feet from the ground. It will

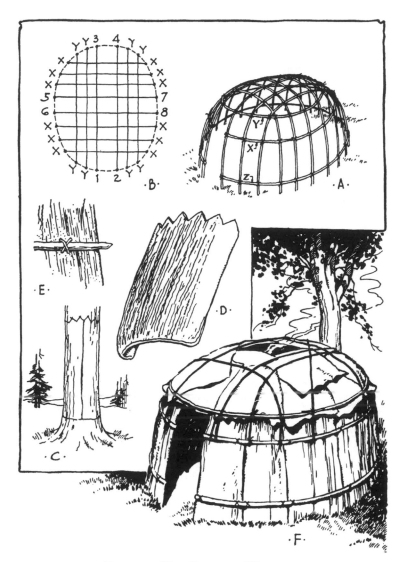

Figure 24. THE CHIPPEWA WAGINOGAN

be noted that X and Z do not extend across the doorway. These poles are lashed to the uprights at each intersection.

The wigwam is now ready for the bark sides.

Gathering the Bark for the Walls.—The sides of the waginogan are covered with rough bark and the roof with birch-bark. For the walls *white cedar* bark is without a peer—it makes a permanent, substantial wall, almost decay-proof, and will withstand the attacks of the climate for years upon years. Among the Chippewas it is always preferred, if obtainable, but lacking this, the following barks are recommended—*ash, spruce, elm, basswood, hemlock* and *chestnut,* the first two being frequently seen on wigwams in the northern country.

Remember that no one has the right to strip bark from trees without the owner's consent unless he is way back in the big woods where the destroying of a few trees will be beneficial to the forest. The taking of cedar or other rough bark promiscuously is in no wise more permissible than such stripping of birch-bark (see page 204). Anyone who is lumbering or cutting trees, or who owns areas soon to be cut, will allow you to take all the bark you need. Under other conditions stripping bark or even hacking into the bark of trees is not only strictly prohibited but is a sort of thing that no one but a blundering tenderfoot would do.

Select big trees with heavy, thick bark, the larger the better—a tree two feet in diameter will provide a sheet of bark measuring about six-and-one-half feet wide when spread out flat. With a hand-ax, cut through the bark around the bottom of the tree, as indicated in C, Figure 24, and again about six feet up or as high as you can reach. This upper cut, which of course will be above one's head, is accomplished by striking with the hand-ax at an angle, forming the zigzag cuts shown in C, Figure 24. Slit the bark between these two cuts and peel off very carefully, thus forming a sheet that will spread out flat into a big shingle like that shown in D, Figure 24. If the bark cannot be loosened from the tree with the use of the fingers and a hand-ax, make a spud from a stick three inches in diameter and two feet long by sharpening one end wedge-shaped. This barking tool is inserted between the bark and the tree trunk and the bark thus pried loose. Cedar will peel easily in the spring and early summer. About twelve or fifteen of these sheets will be needed for the walls, more if the trees are small. Store the bark until needed by stacking it flat on the ground in a shady place, inner side down.

Assembling the Wigwam.—Stand the sheets of cedar bark on end around the sides of the wigwam, letting them rest on the ground and lean against the framework. The zigzag edge of the bark sheet should be up—some writers in describing the wigwams of the Chippewas maintain that the upper edge of the sheet of bark is cut to a zigzag shape in order to make it fit snugly against the frame, but this is scarcely true; the edge of the bark is cut in the zigzag fashion because, as already stated, this is the only way that bark can be cut above the level of one's head in removing it from the tree. The sheets of bark are held in place by the horizontal poles shown in F, Figure 24; these are slender green poles split in half and placed directly parallel to the horizontal poles of the framework behind the bark. Cut small holes through the bark with a knife and lash the outer horizontal poles to the corresponding poles on the inside, as indicated in E, Figure 24. If the sheets of cedar-bark are five feet or more in height, one row of them around the wigwam will make a wall of sufficient height; if they are shorter than this a second layer must be placed above the first and made secure in the same way.

The roof of the wigwam is made of birch-bark stripped from the trees in sheets at least three feet in width (the precautions and instructions in Chapter X should be carefully observed in stripping birch-

Figure 25. BIRCH-BARK STRIPS USED FOR WIGWAM ROOFING

bark). These sheets may be laid over the roof in rather haphazard fashion so as to cover all of the openings and held in place by long strings of basswood-bark or wire, running across the top of the roof and tied to the horizontal poles at the side of the wigwam as shown in F, Figure 24. However, it is much better to lace the sheets of birch-bark into the long strips illustrated in Figure 25 before placing them on the roof. In constructing these, the bark is laced together with well-

soaked thongs of basswood-bark as in making birch-bark baskets—
the instructions for preparing thongs and for lacing are all given in
detail in Chapter X. At each end of these long strips of bark a stick is
lashed as shown in Figure 25, to prevent the bark from splitting and
curling, and at each end of the stick a long string is attached for tying.
Two of these strips ten feet long and six others six feet long will be
needed to make a good roof. Tie the long strips across the top of the
wigwam and attach the shorter strips crosswise to the long ones as
needed to cover the openings, as indicated in Figure 26 which shows
how the roof would appear if one looked down at it from above.

These long strips of birch-bark are to
be preferred to a roof made from many
separate pieces because when so laced
together the bark does not curl, and further because the strips may be removed
from the roof at the end of the season
and rolled up to be saved until the beginning of the next season. The Woodland Indians carry these birch-bark rolls
with them from place to place as they
travel but leave the cedar-bark walls behind, the birch strips being employed for
a number of purposes as occasion demands. One sees rolls of these strips in
the possession of almost every Chippewa
family living in the woods, stacked up
like rolls of carpeting.

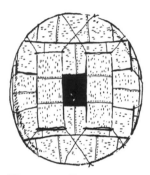

Figure 26. Roof of the
Dome-shaped Wigwam,
Showing Arrangement
of Birch-bark Strips

A hole two feet square is left in the center of the roof to allow the
smoke to escape. A sheet of birch-bark is placed over this hole in
bad weather and tied to the side horizontal holes in the usual fashion.

A blanket is hung over the doorway in bad weather.

The wigwam is now completed except for inside furnishings.
When a fire is built inside, the waginogan becomes as cozy a home
in the woods as one could desire.

Large Wigwams.—If the Indian's family were large he would need
a much more spacious waginogan than the one we have built, but in
making it larger he would not increase it much in width but would
extend it in length. Made wider it would be difficult to heat. In a
long wigwam two fires are sometimes built, one near the front and

the other near the back, each with a smoke hole directly over it in the roof.

In almost every Chippewa village in the northern woods today, one sees the framework of a wigwam measuring 200 feet or more in length, yet not over thirteen feet in width—a long tunnel of arched poles similar to that shown in Figure 27. This is not the framework

Figure 27. FRAME OF THE LODGE OF THE MIDEWIWIN OR GRAND MEDICINE SOCIETY OF THE CHIPPEWAS

of a bark dwelling but rather of the dancing lodge of the Midewiwin or Grand Medicine Society, the ancient religious order of the Chippewas. These frameworks are not covered with bark, but are sided up temporarily when the dances are on by placing pine boughs against the sides to a height of three feet, the boughs being placed with the tops downward. Down and back along the walls of this long-arched tunnel the dancers move in the rites of this most sacred of religious ceremonies.

Wigwam Furnishings.—In the center of the waginogan and directly under the smoke hole is the fireplace. This consists of a square pit three or four inches deep with a frame of logs edged with stones to keep the fire from spreading. Figure 28 shows the arrangement.

Figure 28. WIGWAM FIREPLACE

The right side of the Chippewa wigwam, as one enters the door, is reserved for the men of the family and the left side for the women. The father's sitting and sleeping place is just to the right of the entrance with his sons located on the right side farther back from him, while the mother sits and sleeps to the left of the entrance with her daughters next to her. With this arrangement the young folks must pass the mother and father in leaving the wigwam. The place of honor in the wigwam is at the rear opposite the entrance—this is reserved for the grandmother and grandfather. In case there are no grandparents this area is left vacant so far as sleeping quarters are concerned, but the medicine bags and family sacred bundles are kept there.

A bench which is used for sleeping at night and for a shelf in the daytime is built all the way around the edge of the wigwam about a foot and a half from the floor.

The bench is made by lashing poles with strings of basswood bark to a supporting frame. At night the beds are made by placing a mat of bulrushes over the bench on top of which balsam, hemlock or cedar boughs are

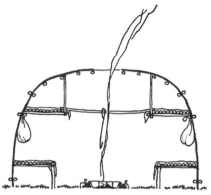

Figure 29. INTERIOR OF THE WAGINOGAN

placed as a soft mattress for the blankets. In the daytime the boughs and blankets are rolled up in the mat and shoved under the bench. Often waginogans are seen which have no benches of this type, the family making their beds on the bulrush mats placed on the floor, so arranged in cold weather that the folks sleep with their feet toward the fire. It will be seen in Figure 29, which shows the interior of the wigwam, that storage shelves are also placed near the roof of the wigwam, made as always by lashing poles together with basswood-bark thongs. A pothook usually made of

Figure 30. PLATFORMS BUILT OUTSIDE THE WAGINOGAN

chokecherry is suspended over the fire on which to hang kettles, sometimes attached to a pole between the shelves as shown in

Figure 29, and sometimes suspended from one of the upper poles of the wigwam by a cord of basswood-bark.

Outside the wigwam and attached to one side of it (usually the right side as one faces the door) is a platform with a roof over it as shown in Figure 30. Under this platform wood is stored, and on it the women sit in pleasant weather making birch-bark makuks and sewing moccasins, or doing whatever task the day's work demands. Sometimes the roof of this platform consists merely of green boughs for shade but more often it is made of poles fashioned into a platform that makes a handy storage shelf.

The floor of the waginogan around the fire is kept immaculately clean by the women. The ashes are removed each day and the dirt floor swept with a broom made of shavings or grass. The ground is sprinkled with water frequently which in time causes it to become firmly packed and as solid and smooth as if made of concrete.

Substitutes for Bark.—Today one frequently sees Indian wigwams with tar-paper roofs in areas where birch-bark is no longer to be found. While the black tar-paper makes a serviceable roof, needless to say it is somber, ugly and uninviting as compared to the birch-bark. In fact, the whole framework of the wigwam may be covered with tar-paper for summer use if nothing better can be obtained.

For use in a summer camp, or for exhibition purposes, the framework of poles may be covered with canvas strips which if carefully prepared will make a most attractive wigwam, even if an unauthentic one. Measure the circumference of the wigwam at the bottom and cut two strips of yard-wide canvas to this length, putting grommets one foot apart at the ends, and two feet apart along the side. Run one of these strips of canvas around the bottom of the wigwam, tying it with strings through the grommets to the poles of the framework at the top and to tent pegs at the bottom. Then place the second layer of canvas around the wigwam above the first, overlapping it six inches. Now several shorter strips of canvas six feet long should be placed across the roof and tied just as in the case of the birch-bark strips. The usual smoke hole should be left in the roof and a square of canvas provided to cover it in rainy weather.

A combination of bark and canvas may be used to good advantage, making the walls of cedar-bark as usual and using canvas instead of birch-bark for the roof.

Bark Tepees

The out-post home of the roving Woodland Indians in the summer was the pointed bark tepee or *nasa-ogan*, and it makes a good, practical summer home today for anyone finding it necessary to fashion a shelter in the deep woods in which he is to live for some time. Quicker and easier of construction than the waginogan, it was the favorite shelter for the Indian family when moving from place to place—frequently a family would have several of these tepee frames in various places in the woods, waiting only for the bark to make them habitable—one at the spring maple-sugaring grounds, one at the summer blueberry fields, one at the autumn wild-rice marshes, and so forth. The bark tepee is lacking in warmth alongside the waginogan (but of what concern is warmth in the summer?), but a fire may be built inside for cheer and coziness, and enough of the smoke will remain within to free the place of the insect pests that so often turn a pleasant summer evening into a nightmare.

There are two types of bark tepees prevalent in the Chippewa country, the temporary one of very quick construction which is to be used only for a short time, and a permanent type designed to stand for years as an out-camp for summer use. Let us describe the permanent one first.

Permanent Bark Tepees.—Sixteen poles, each eighteen feet long, are needed for the frame. Mark a circle on the ground about twelve feet in diameter and set up the poles into the pyramid shown in A, Figure 31, using the same method of erecting and tying described for the canvas tepee (see pages 28 and 29). The bark for the walls is gathered in large sheets just as for the waginogan (page 43), using *white cedar* if obtainable, otherwise *spruce, elm, hemlock, ash,* or *basswood.* The slabs are set on end around the framework and held in place with slender split poles as shown in E, Figure 31. Bend one sapling around the bottom about four inches from the ground, cut small holes through the bark directly over the upright poles within, and lash the outside horizontal sapling to the inner uprights with basswood-bark thongs or wire. Now put a second tier of bark above the lower, overlapping it a few inches, and fasten with a split pole as before. A third tier is then put on in order to bring the cedar bark up to within about four feet of the peak. A space a little over two feet in width is left for a doorway.

Figure 31. THE BARK TEPEE OF THE WOODLAND INDIANS

One of the long birch-bark strips shown in D, Figure 31, must now be made for the peak, measuring three feet in width and about twelve feet in length, constructed according to the directions given on page 44. Put this strip in place around the peak and tie as shown in E. The birch-bark strip is shifted from side to side as the wind changes to draw out the smoke: it is placed on the side of the lodge against which the wind is blowing, leaving the opposite side more open.

The methods of handling the birch and cedar-bark, and the details of construction are all similar to those used in making a bark wigwam, and the detailed description of wigwam construction should be read for a full explanation.

Temporary or Make-Shift Bark Tepees.—More commonly seen than the well-built tepee just described is the make-shift one shown in

Figure 32. TEMPORARY BARK TEPEE

Figure 32, which is understandable because the tepee is almost always employed as a temporary dwelling. The pyramid of poles is set up as before except that it has a wider diameter at the base—perhaps sixteen feet—with the result that the sides have a more gradual slope. Cover the sides of the framework with loose pieces of bark of any size or shape, and of any kind, using any pieces that can be found, beginning at the bottom and working up, laying the bark on shingle-fashion. Hold these pieces in place by leaning poles against the walls as shown in the drawing—there are then two rows of poles around the tepee, the inner pyramid and those of the outer row which merely lean against the walls. By using these poles to hold the walls there is no time wasted in lacing and tying the bark, or in cutting sheets of bark to uniform size. Furthermore, the tepee can be dismantled for moving in short order by merely throwing down the outside poles and stacking up the bark.

TEPEES FOR SHADE ONLY

In our manner of living the porch provides a cool, shaded place for the summer days, and awnings keep out the scorching rays of the sun. In the Indian villages of the woods it is an open tepee frame with a covering on one side that brings comfort and coolness during the long summer days. Outside the bark waginogan, or near the present-day Indian's log hut, we find the family sitting in the shade of one of these open tepees, making makuks, sewing on moccasins, tying up fishnets, or just sitting and talking—or perhaps the men folks are

Figure 33. A TEPEE FOR SHADE ONLY

gathered there in a little huddle playing the moccasin game to the drumming of the moccasin drum. These are practical shelters for a summer camp—if a bark waginogan is used as the headquarters of the campcraft and the woodcraft departments (and could a structure be found that more appropriately fits these activities?), an open tepee for shade nearby gives the campers a pleasant, woodsy place to work on their crafts.

Erect the usual pyramid of poles, using a dozen or sixteen slender saplings sixteen feet long, spreading them wide at the bottom into a circle at least sixteen feet in diameter, thus giving the walls a low slant. There are several ways of shading the circle: A piece of *canvas* ten by twelve feet in size may be placed over the side from which the sun is coming, with ropes attached to each corner with which to tie it to the poles. Often the Indians of today employ canvas in this way, but the old-timers and those in the far woods still use the *birch-bark strips* made as illustrated in D, Figure 31 and described on page 44, which they roll up like carpeting at night and spread over the frame in the daytime. Or a few *leafy boughs* are cut and laid against the poles as in Figure 33, to be replaced by others when they become wilted. As the direction of the sun changes, the boughs, canvas, or bark can be shifted accordingly.

BARK HOUSES

Rare as compared to the wigwam and the tepee, among those Indians who looked to bark for their shelters, are the bark houses

Figure 34. A PEAKED BARK HOUSE

with peaked roofs, yet occasionally one is seen in the Chippewa country. Figure 34 shows the more common of these bark houses—it's really an elongated tepee, with the front and back walls semi-circular in shape at the bottom, each comprising half of a tepee, the two halves separated by a ridge pole. The large sheets of birch-bark are laid on the frame shingle-fashion, beginning at the bottom and working up, and are held in place by poles laid against the sides as in making the temporary tepee described in the preceding section.

Another type of the Woods Indian bark house is shown in Figure

35—a low structure with walls not over five feet high. The framework is built of slender poles without the use of nails, the fastenings being made with lashings of basswood bark. The walls are made of cedar, spruce, or elm bark, set up and held in place as in making a bark wigwam, and the roof is made either of cedar or birch-bark, preferably the latter, held in place with long strings of basswood bark as in tying down the roof of a dome-shaped wigwam.

Figure 35. AN INDIAN BARK HOUSE

BIRCH-BARK SHINGLES

The finest shingles in the world are the sheets of thick, waterproof and decay-proof birch-bark—they will long outlive the logs of the building on which they are placed—but the scarcity of bark as compared to wood argues emphatically against their general use as roofing shingles on cabins unless one is forced to it away back in the bush.

I have seen square frame houses built by the northern Woodland Indians in recent years which were covered completely, both walls and roof, with birch-bark slabs tacked to the siding and roofing boards. Instead of overlapping the sheets on the side walls like shingles, a neater effect can be produced by fitting the edges of the sheets together evenly and then covering the cracks with inch-wide twigs split in half.

The picturesque, woodsy appearance of these little houses covered with beautiful birch-bark stand out in distinct contrast to the ugliness of the frame shacks covered with tar-paper which one sees so often in northern Indian villages today—but one cannot blame the Indians in these areas for resorting to black tar-paper, for we have stolen the birch trees from them. Nothing is more certain than the fact that they would welcome a return to the old life if by some miracle the beautiful forests could be returned to them.

BARK LEAN-TOS

We have already seen that a temporary lean-to for a few days of camping may be quickly thrown together from bark (Figure 4 on page 8), but in Figure 36 we have a substantial one that will withstand the tempest for many years with a little annual repair. This makes an excellent open shelter of the ideal type with a roof at the proper angle to catch the heat of the reflector fire built in front, but it demands almost as much work as building a bark wigwam or tepee, and offers less actual shelter; the average person wishing to go to this much trouble would probably prefer to make a waginogan, but there are many who prefer the open lean-to for camping purposes and if you are one of these and plan to remain at the same spot for sometime, here is the lean-to de luxe.

The framework is shown in A, Figure 36, the uprights being crotched sticks driven into the ground. If birch-bark is available, lace

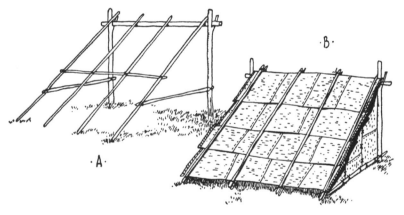

Figure 36. A SUBSTANTIAL BARK LEAN-TO

the pieces together into strips as long as the lean-to is wide, following the method described on page 44 and illustrated in Figure 25. Place these crosswise of the lean-to beginning at the bottom and overlapping shingle-fashion. Tie the ends to the end poles, and weight the strips down in the middle with poles, as shown in Figure 36, tied at the top and bottom to the underlying poles of the framework. The side walls are made of bark laced together and tied to the supporting framework.

If birch-bark is not available one of the following barks may be used: *cedar, spruce, hemlock, basswood, ash, or chestnut.* In using these the rough outer bark should be removed, leaving only the fibrous inner bark. While the neatest job would be obtained by soaking the bark for a few days and then pulling loose the inner layer from the outer, the element of time usually necessitates merely the scraping off of the thickest of the outer bark with a hand-ax until it is reasonably smooth—this will make a passably presentable lean-to and every bit as serviceable a one. If the bark is taken from big trees, two feet or more in diameter, the sheets will be seven feet or more in width and thus sufficiently wide to cover the length of the average lean-to without splicing. Remember never to strip bark without the consent of the owner of the land.

CHAPTER IV

PERMANENT TOMAHAWK SHELTERS

THE TIMBER Indians of long years past with naught but implements of stone and bone found bark within their easy grasp but logs in quantities for shelters a little too forbidding. Came the metal tomahawk and the ax in later times but the bark tradition still lingered and even to this day the waginogans and nasa-ogans of the last chapter provide the favored summer home.

Products of a different culture were the white pioneers, trappers, and loggers who invaded the woods, and applying their intelligence to the hewing of an existence from the wilds, developed many and sundry shelters out of their axmanship.

Each of these backgrounds, the red and the white, has given us types of camps and lodges that have withstood the test of years by those to whom living meant camping. The red we have discussed and now we approach the white. But be it remembered that the full-grown axmanship of the pioneer as manifested in his log cabins is beyond the scope of our present picture, for ours is the task of wielding the tomahawk, the young-sized camp-ax, in the fashioning of the more permanent and substantial of the trail shelters. True, we may employ the full ax at times, as in splitting slabs and in cutting heavier poles, but all to the end of shelters no more pretentious than the lean-to type.

First, shelters made of slabs and then of logs:

SLAB SHELTERS

There is many and many a good shelter in the pile of slabs out behind the old sawmill, waiting to be erected by someone who wants a lean-to in the woods. There is nothing second-rate about a good slab lean-to—simple as it is to make, it does its work as well as does a log shelter, and it looks right in the woods. Perhaps a good load of the slabs can be hauled from the sawmill to the location, these to be sorted over, saving the better ones for the shelter, and condemning the rest to firewood. A sawmill near a summer camp is a valuable asset for there are many uses for these slabs in campcraft and woodcraft, other than for shelter building, and a goodly supply should be laid in at the beginning of the season—they are inexpensive material for projects in that they have scant market value.

Too much reliance should not be placed in these sawmill slabs in camps for boys, however, for these young woodsmen should learn how to split slabs from logs with ax and wedge, which is the task that would confront one if he wished a slab camp in the far wilds. The best woods for slab splitting are cedar, spruce, pine, basswood, ash, or chestnut. See Chapter VII for the methods of splitting.

Figure 37. A QUICK LEAN-TO OF SLABS

A QUICK SLAB LEAN-TO

Merely leaning the slabs against a cross-pole as in Figure 37 will produce a fair enough shelter for a few nights of camping. Drive two forked sticks in the ground for the cross-pole or tie it firmly to two trees. Using nine-foot slabs, lay one layer against the pole as in the illustration with the flat sides up, and then lay another course over these with the flat sides down, the slabs in the second layer being so arranged as to cover the cracks in the lower. That is all that is necessary for a few days camping—it will take a pretty stiff wind to lift these slabs off the pole, and a bitterly cold night to make the camper uncomfortable if he has a blazing fire in front built as it should be in reflector fashion. If deemed wise, the shelter can be made more durable by digging a little trench in which the lower ends of the slabs will rest to prevent them from slipping downward (this ditch will also serve for drainage) and further, by spiking the slabs to the ridgepole or lashing them either by running a basswood-bark thong across the top of the lean-to and tying it to the uprights, or by placing a slender pole across the upper end and lashing the ends of it to the uprights.

A Substantial Slab Shelter

If you have a favorite trout-fishing pool a day's journey back into the bush at which you want a handy permanent shelter, here is one quick of construction that looks the part of a woodsman. And if a group of boys or the campers of an organized camp have a favorite out-camp to which they often go, here is the shelter they themselves can build. If groups of more than four or five campers are to frequent the spots, however, the slab shelter next described—that of the Adirondack style—should be preferred.

The camp we are to build is pictured in Figure 38, from which anyone can easily figure out the method of construction except for one unique feature of slab construction—the grooves or scooped-out troughs that run the length of the bottom roof slabs: It will be noted that there are two layers of slabs on the roof, the bottom course placed with the flat sides up, and the upper layer with the flat sides down, so spaced that the upper slabs cover the cracks in the lower course. Down the middle of the flat side of each of the lower slabs a shallow trough is chopped out, thus creating a ditch right under the edges of the upper slabs down which the rainwater drains. Minus these gutters no amount of careful fitting of the slabs will serve to shed a heavy shower. These troughs may be quickly dispatched by hacking a series of crosswise cuts a few inches apart down the middle of the plank with an ax, and then cleaning the wood out between them with gentle lengthwise chops.

A device often used in this type of roof is to place poles between the lower slabs as in E, Figure 38; this separates the lower slabs enough so that the edges of the upper slabs just reach the gutter, and at the same time gives the roof rigidity and prevents the slabs from warping and sagging.

Although not absolutely essential, a good-sized log makes an excellent foundation for the back of the shack. The front cross-pole should be firmly spiked to substantial uprights, with two side poles connecting it with the back log to serve as supports to which the side slabs are nailed. To serve best the bottoms of the side slabs should be

Figure 38. A SUBSTANTIAL SLAB SHELTER

nailed to large logs ten to twelve inches thick, laid along the inside, these logs to make the additional contribution of seats for the campers. Tradition demands that across the front of every open camp of this sort a large log at least twelve inches in diameter be placed to serve as the *deacon's seat.* Thus we have a foundation of four heavy logs in the recommended camp, as will be seen in C, Figure 38, all of which might be omitted and still produce a substantial shelter if lack of time and material so dictates. The cracks in the shelter may be chinked with moss.

A Slab Camp of the Adirondack Type

Minus logs with which to construct a standard Adirondack lean-to, slabs may be employed to a better advantage than one might imagine, and although an imitation that no one would prefer to the real article unless necessary, they do produce a substantial shelter that looks the part of the ever-popular Adirondack.

A framework of substantial poles must be built to the plan shown

Figure 39. Frame for a Slab Lean-to of the Adirondack Type

in Figure 39, the ground plan measuring eight by twelve feet, the front elevation seven feet and the back elevation three-and-one-half feet. Nail the roof slabs in place in two layers, using slabs that have been scooped out or grooved with drainage troughs as described for the preceding lean-to. The same type of roof is continued down in front to form the apron. This apron extends out three feet and has the same slope as the roof. The side and back slabs are nailed vertically in two layers as in laying the roof. A little chinking of clay or moss may be necessary to fill the cracks. And don't forget the deacon's seat across the front opening.

THE ADIRONDACK LOG LEAN-TO

Somewhere there is a secluded spot deep in the wilds beside a little lake or stream where you should have a permanent shelter that will forever beckon and urge you to come and camp and enjoy true sanctuary. Perhaps you cannot get there often enough to justify a log cabin—or the spot may be a few hours' paddle away from the wood-

land cabin that is already yours. There you should build an Adirondack open camp—a sturdy, woodsy log lean-to of quick construction
as log building goes, yet of generous proportions and full of coziness.
The memories of nights spent there in the open, precious as they may
be, will scarcely equal those of the building of the camp—the busy,
happy days of hauling and notching and chinking will be a joy forever.

Log construction in true pioneer fashion is the best of rugged experience for anyone, particularly boys. Better by far than the making
of trinkets of metal and leather in a summer camp is the building with
logs—the swinging of axes, the wielding of cant-hooks, the pounding
of wedges, the driving of twelve-inch spikes, the lifting, the hauling. . . .

A shelter is being built, but that is only a by-product in the building of men, for

> "We are all blind until we see
> That in the human plan
> Nothing is worth the making if
> It does not make the man."
> —Edwin Markham.

The experience gained in fashioning a log lean-to may pave the
way to attempting a full-grown log cabin, for the principles of notching and handling logs are the same regardless of the size of the structure.

Traditional styles of shelters vary in different parts of the country.
The one we are considering has been labeled as the *Adirondack*
lean-to because of its long-continued and ever-increasing popularity
in the northeastern states, particularly in the Adirondacks, where it is
to be found along all the trails and portages, ready and waiting for
any weary traveler that seeks its shelter. Today it is far from a provin-
cial, northeastern structure for it has been accepted across the land as
the best of open camps, combining the fascination and charm of living
in the open with ideal protection from the weather. With a reflector
fire in front it becomes a huge reflecting baker—the sloping roof
catches the heat and throws it downward producing a coziness in
zero weather excelling the comfort of closed shacks and draughty
cabins. It is a most satisfactory protection from the cold, an excellent

shelter from the wet, provides plenty of fresh air, and enables you to see the cheery blaze of the campfire—could one ask more?

MAKING THE OPEN LOG CAMP

Any kind of softwood logs that can be obtained near the site of the shelter may be used, the best of the woods for log construction being *spruce, cedar, pine, balsam, hemlock* and *chestnut*. Hardwood is much too heavy to handle and difficult to work. If very short-lived woods such as basswood, cottonwood, willow and aspen must be used (see page 73), the poles should be heavily stained or creosoted for protection from dampness. Good straight poles about six to eight inches in diameter will be needed, together with four heavier ones for the bottom course and some slender stuff for rafters.

A rugged open camp such as this is unquestionably more attractive if made of logs with the bark left on, but bark holds moisture that leads to rapid decay and gives boring insects a home while doing their destructive work. The choice must be made between a rough-and-ready, woods-like camp of relatively short life, and a trim, peeled-log one of long duration. The rawness of new peeled logs may be relieved by a little stain. If the logs are to be peeled, they should be cut during the spring months or at least before midsummer, at which time of year they will peel easily, but thereafter only with extreme difficulty. They should be hauled to location before peeling else they will be too slippery to handle. A barking-spud will rip off the bark in short order if it is "running good," and if it binds in spots a draw-knife will relieve it.

Lay two skid poles on the ground and pile the logs neatly on them to facilitate handling and selecting—this is called the *skid pile*.

In selecting the site, the camp should be faced so that *the open side is protected at least in part from the prevailing winds*, even if the best view of the scenery is sacrificed thereby—this is an important matter for one will have no zest for beautiful landscapes with the full blast of a gale driving broadside into the opening.

The best size for an open camp is 8 by 12 feet. These shelters may vary from 7 by 10 feet up to 13 by 16 feet but sizes larger than 8 by 12 are not recommended owing to increased difficulties in heating—if larger groups must be accommodated it is better to construct two adjoining shelters. Stake out the cabin and stretch chalk lines between the stakes. Make sure you have it square by the following method:

Figure 40. THE ADIRONDACK LOG LEAN-TO

Figure 41. ADIRONDACK OPEN CAMP WITH LOG-CABIN CORNERS

mark a point six feet from the stake on one line and eight feet on the other line, then measure diagonally between these two points—the distance should reach exactly ten feet.

The only really essential tools needed are an ax, a hand-ax, a hammer, a cedar saw or one-man crosscut saw, a two-inch chisel, and

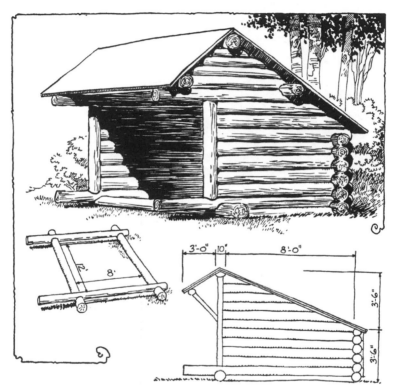

Figure 42. PLAN OF THE ADIRONDACK LEAN-TO

a gouge of similar width. In addition, however, a square, a level, and a drawknife will come in handy.

Put large stones at each corner to serve as a foundation. Select the largest logs for the bottom course—four of them because in this bottom course there is to be a log across the open side of the lean-to as in Figure 42 to serve as the *deacon's seat.* And the deacon is entitled to recline on the best log in the outfit, a straight smooth one at least twelve inches in diameter. Lay it and its mate to the rear first, fit two six-inch end logs in between them as in Figure 42 and then lay the two main end logs, notching them with a curved or U-shaped notch to fit over the lower front and back logs. If these two large end logs are allowed to extend a good eighteen inches out in front as in the drawing, they will make excellent seats. With the bottom course of logs in place, snap a chalk line down the middle of each and measure again to see if the foundation is square.

Now a decision must be reached as to the type of front corner desired. There are four possible selections, all illustrated in Figure 43. The most picturesque and appropriate is the log-cabin corner in A

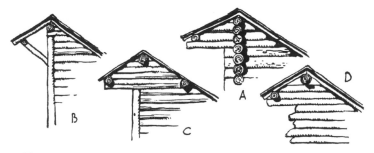

Figure 43. FOUR TYPES OF CORNERS FOR THE OPEN LOG LEAN-TO

made with short cross-logs notched in the usual log-cabin manner, but this is extravagant both in time and materials as compared to the other types. If it is used the ends of the logs may be sawed square in uniform lengths as in A, or left roughly chopped at irregular lengths with artistic effect. The easiest and most economical corner is shown in B—the ends of the logs are sawed square and a split log nailed vertically to them. A similar arrangement of better appearance is seen in C. In D we have a deliberate attempt at a crude, unfinished effect—in fact there is no finished corner at all but the logs are left at irregular lengths and with no apparent support; such a lean-to gives a feeling of distress for fear the logs will suddenly roll asunder, although of course long spikes hold everything secure. In all of these types, the back corners are notched in log-cabin fashion.

The second and all succeeding courses of logs are laid just as the first, with unusual care given to the notching following the instructions on notching in the section following in this chapter. After each log is in place it should be spiked to the one below it with twelve-inch spikes.

The back elevation is three-and-one-half feet. Above this the side logs should have one end chopped to a slant to fit the slope of the roof. The side logs continue up to the peak of the gable, each one fitted and spiked to the log below. The height of the ridgepole is seven feet from the floor.

As the walls go up constant care must be exercised to see that they are vertical—this is accomplished by vertical pencil lines drawn on the ends of the logs before the notching is done as described in detail in the discussion of notching which follows this section. One must be on the alert also to see that the walls are level: The ends of the logs should be reversed, the small end of each log placed over the butt end of the log beneath it. Check occasionally by laying a board on the top log and placing a level on it.

If the front corner is of the type shown in B and C, Figure 43, a finishing upright slab consisting of a log split in half should be spiked to the ends of the logs. The flat side of this slab should be hewed smooth and the ends of the logs sawed square to fit it snugly.

A six-inch log is used for the ridgepole, firmly spiked to the top of the upright slab at each front corner. The rafters run from the ridgepole to the back wall and extend a foot beyond it. These poles should be about four inches thick at the big end and should be spaced eighteen inches, nine in all being needed for a shack twelve feet long. The large end of the rafters should be toward the ridgepole. The roof boards are nailed across these rafters, running lengthwise of the shelter and extending a foot beyond the ends.

Another type of rafter arrangement commonly seen is made by placing a six-inch log parallel to the ridgepole midway between it and the back wall—this method is used in the cabin in Figure 42. In this case the roof boards should be nailed in the sloping position at right angles to the ridge.

The apron extends out in front two-and-one-half to three feet and has the same slope as the roof itself. If the arrangement shown in B, Figure 43, is used, nine apron rafters will be needed to be attached to the ridgepole where they meet the roof rafters. The bottom ends of these are nailed to a four- or five-inch pole which is supported at each end by a brace nailed to the upright at the front corner.

If lumber is not available for the roof, small poles may be fitted close together and the tops leveled off to a reasonably smooth surface, or shakes may be split from logs.

Roofing may be homemade shingles or commercial shingles, composition roofing, or even tar-paper. One of the most popular commercial roofings for open camps is the patented asphalt type with a top of crushed slate.

The warmest place to sleep in one of these open shelters is as near the floor as possible, and if the camp is so situated that the floor is reasonably free from dampness a bunk may be built of poles and lumber just off the ground. The bunk should extend entirely across the back and since one sleeps warmer if his feet are toward the fire, it should extend out from the back wall six-and-one-half feet. A bunk of this size built just off the ground really constitutes a floor, and so it is well to extend the boards all the way up to the deacon's seat, placing a pole across six-and-one-half feet for the back to terminate the bunk in case boughs are used for bedding. Should the camp give promise of dampness the bunk should be elevated eighteen inches and built lengthwise of the cabin along the back wall, extending out the width of the bunk—two bunks will be possible, each six feet long, separated in the middle by a board. This arrangement has the advantage of leaving the main floor of the camp open for general use.

Shelves can be built around the side and back walls and spikes driven in the logs to serve as hooks.

<h2 style="text-align:center">NOTCHING</h2>

The three common methods of cornering in log construction are shown in A, B and C, Figure 44. A departure from pioneer methods is seen in D, but this modern device is scarcely recommended in log cabins or lean-tos.

By all odds the best type of notching, and the one we shall describe in detail, is the round or U-shaped notch shown in A. It will be noted that the logs are notched on the lower side only, this notch fitting over the log below it. Let us assume that the lower course of four logs is in place on the foundation of the lean-to. Place the first log of the second course in its position and when it has been trued up and lies directly over the log beneath it, draw a perpendicular line

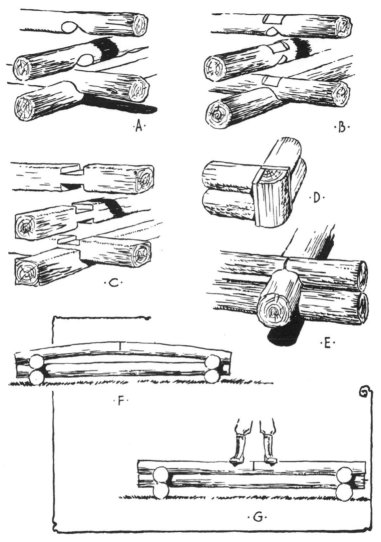

Figure 44. METHODS OF NOTCHING, SPLICING AND STRAIGHTENING LOGS

with a pencil down the middle of its end. And also mark on its underside the width of the crosswise log below it over which the notch is
to fit. Then roll the log over on its back, using a cant-hook if necessary, and chop the notch out roughly with a hand-ax. Roll the log
back into position and test the notch for size, then turn it back again
and continue chopping it out and smoothing it up with a two-inch
gouge. It will be necessary to roll it into position several times to
check the progress of the notch. When finished it should fit very
snugly and should allow the log to drop flush with the lengthwise
log beneath it. Furthermore, when the notch is completed the perpendicular line on the end of the log should still be perpendicular
to the ground. When both ends of the log are notched and the log
is finally in position, a twelve-inch spike should be driven through
each notch into the log beneath with additional spikes at intervals of
six feet along its length.

The purpose of the vertical line at the end of the log is to assist
in keeping the walls perpendicular as the logs go up. As each succeeding log is notched and put in position, the vertical line on its end
should be a continuation of the lines on the logs beneath.

It sometimes happens that one is forced to use a log that tapers
down to too small an end to look well when notched and in position.
A clever device to relieve this is to splice on a larger end as shown in
E, Figure 44. The end of the log is sawed off directly in the middle
of the notch and the larger butt is spliced on by spiking it onto the
crosswise log beneath. When the corner has been completed it is very
difficult to detect the presence of this splicing, and the corner takes
on a much neater appearance than it would have had if the small end
had been allowed to remain.

There are two ways to trim the logs at the corners: One is to saw
them off to uniform length a foot to fifteen inches out from the
corner. Or, they may be left at irregular lengths, some much longer
than others, with the ends either sawed or roughly chopped. Which
of these two methods should be used is a matter of personal taste—one
produces a neat, ship-shape job while the other gives a rough-and-
ready backwoods atmosphere.

Straightening Crooked Logs

The ideal logs for construction purposes are straight and smooth
with as little taper as possible, but sometimes the skid pile will not

produce enough of these to complete the shelter and we are forced to use an occasional crooked one. But this should not cause undue worry for the crook can be easily taken out so as to produce a straight, smooth pole. The log should be placed on the wall with the bulge up and notched in the usual way, then spiked permanently in position. Saw part way through the log at the highest point of the crook with a crosscut saw as indicated in F, Figure 44. Now if you stand on the log with one foot each side of the sawed cut, your weight will force it down. If it is still crooked saw it again making the cut a little wider. When it's forced down far enough to be satisfactory spike it to the log below with a twelve-inch spike each side of the cut. No one looking at the finished pole would suspect that it was other than a straight pole when hauled to position.

CHINKING AND CAULKING

If the logs fit very close together the narrow cracks may be caulked with damp moss, preferably sphagnum moss, or with oakum. These materials are forced into the cracks from both sides of the logs with a caulking iron or wooden wedge, driven with a mallet. If the cracks are wide it may be necessary to close them with lengths of quartered logs shaped to fit the cracks, bedded in clay or mortar and nailed.

Clay makes a very good caulking and one that will stand up ten to fifteen years if well done. The clay should be mixed with water to the consistency of putty and forced into the cracks.

Mortar makes the most enduring and watertight chinking. Where the cracks are wide metal laths or meshed wire made for the purpose should be nailed in them before the mortar is applied in order to give it a foundation. A mixture of cement mortar and wood-pulp plaster makes the best caulking, the latter substance giving the mortar more consistency for filling the larger openings between the logs—cement mortar alone is inclined to be too runny and has a tendency to settle away from the log above as it dries. It is well to apply the mortar thicker where it rests on the lower log allowing it to taper to the log above, thus giving the caulking a wider base at the bottom and preventing its settling. If the logs are allowed to season before they are caulked, they will not shrink away from the mortar.

Resistance of Woods to Decay

If the knowledge of any one quality of woods is more valuable than another in log construction, it is resistance to decay when exposed to the weather or in contact with the ground. Some woods are so perishable they will rot away in a few months whereas others are famed for their durability. If you plant a post of sugar maple, which is a hard, strong and tough wood, the chances are that before another year rolls around a good push with the hand will send it toppling down, rotted away quite completely at the ground level. But if this same pole were of white cedar, a comparatively soft, light, and weak wood, it would stand strong and sturdy when tested several years hence.

Exposure to alternate wetting and drying is the condition under which decay takes place most rapidly. All posts erected in the ground and all poles having contact with the ground must be of durable woods. In the upper courses of a cabin or lean-to we may safely use certain kinds of poles that would tend to decay quickly if placed on or near the ground. Particular care is necessary in the selection of logs for the foundation and lower course.

Here are the relative merits of some of the more common woods east of the Rockies in respect to decay, the common trees not listed being regarded as having less resistance to decay than white oak:

Woods Very Resistant to Decay

Catalpa
Cedars
Chestnut
Cypress
Locust, Black
Walnut

Woods Resistant to Decay

Butternut
Locust, Honey
Oak, White
Persimmon
Sycamore

Woods With Moderate Resistance to Decay

Elm, Rock
Gum, Red
Pine, Pitch
"   White
"   Yellow
Tamarack
Tulip-tree (Yellow Poplar)
Sassafras

Woods That Decay Quickly

Ash, White
Beech
Birch, Paper
"   Yellow
Elm, White
Hemlock
Maple, Sugar
Oak, Red
Pine, Lodgepole
"   Norway
Spruces

Woods That Decay Very Quickly

Aspen
Basswood
Cottonwood
Fir, Balsam
Gum, Black
Pine, Jack
Poplar
Willow

CHAPTER V

BEDS AND DUFFEL

THERE ARE two types of tenderfeet, one less annoying than the other because the first is merely innocent while the second is either an impractical dreamer, inexperienced in the woods, or is an insincere bluffer, mostly the latter, because he bobs up everywhere in the city but seldom in the woods, boasting outrageously of his toughness on the trail.

Our innocent tenderfoot means well and tries hard, much too hard because the load of unnecessary duffel he tries to haul into the woods would cause a good-sized pack-mule to sit down and rebel. Some of this breed are gadget buyers, sold on the indispensable usefulness of every camping knickknack they see—and the outfitting stores are crammed with possibilities. The more of these gewgaws they move into the woods the better costumed they feel themselves to be for the role they are trying to play. But others, and these are the majority, sincerely try to make up a good outfit but take far and away too much stuff, most of which will never be used.

Not so with tenderfoot No. 2—he is the he-man of the wilds. He takes little or nothing because camping is roughing it—and being the he-man that he is he can "take it." The rocks are never too hard beneath his blankets nor the steak too raw or burnt to suit his taste! When on rare occasion one of these tough gentlemen is come upon in the woods, it is surprising to see how quickly his barking subsides as the hardships resulting from his inadequate equipment take their toll. But once back in his easy chair at home, his ruggedness quickly returns as he recounts his deeds.

No true camper thinks in terms of hardships or inconvenience. The

74

more experienced he is the more he insists on comfort. The veteran knows too well the trials of the trail to go unprepared and, moreover, he knows too well the burden of an overheavy pack to take an ounce of unnecessary duffel.

I have two old friends very wise in the ways of the woods who have demonstrated that it is possible to live without equipment in the wilds. To see if it could be done, one went into the bush with gun, knife, and ax to stay three months, removed his clothing and proceeded to secure materials, fashion clothing and moccasins, find food, bedding and covering—and he returned at the end of the three months well and happy but recommending stoutly that when you go camping you should go well equipped for every emergency! The other is an old Rocky Mountain guide and prospector who knows those mountains like a map. With only his gun and a bag of salt, he departed into the ranges for a year, ran amuck with a grizzly bear and was laid up unable to walk for three months. But came the year's end and he strolled out none the worse! Now both of these men were fortified by years of training, and were merely experimenting. Today both are the strongest advocates of ample camping equipment, both for themselves and for others.

To attempt to emulate the Indian who did much with little presupposes the Indian's training and this we do not have today, not even the most experienced of us. The eastern Woodland Indians trained their children long and well for the wilderness life. To a certain spot in the woods they would send them with instructions to make camp, strip, kill certain animals, make moccasins and clothing, kill a deer, and return with it to the village. If they were too long about it or they did their work poorly, they would be sent out again to repeat. But this was for schooling—the adult Indian knew what to take along and took it.

Now both of our types of tenderfeet will learn if they camp long enough. On each succeeding trip we will find the first type taking less and less as he proves the worthlessness and uselessness of this item and that, until at last he settles down to the outfit that is at once light and adequate. And a trip or two should convince the second type that he is worshiping the wrong god if he thinks that camping is synonymous with roughing it.

The art of packing is to have everything you need when you need it and not be burdened with one item you do not need. The trails are too long, the hills too steep, the portages too rough—it is brutal to torture yourself with overheavy packs. There is truth in the old proverb that an ounce in the morning is a pound before night. We *must* go light. But the trails will be shorter, the hills less high, and the going less rough if we have the necessary equipment to live in *comfort*.

In buying equipment it is well to equip for two rather than one. For example, it is usually a mistake to purchase a one-man tent for seldom will you go alone and you will have no hospitality for an invited companion. Get a two-man tent. The same applies to the cooking outfit—a one-man outfit is inadequate even for one man and it leaves no chance to entertain a companion. A two-man outfit weighs less than two one-man outfits and when there are two in the party, there are two backs to carry the load.

First, let us consider the important question of bedding, and then discuss packs and general duffel.

WOODLAND BEDS

One thing is certain, the Angel of the Night will never hover over one's tent with her matchless blessing of calm, sweet sleep, the woodland's perfect rest, if one is lying with a rock in his back and a prong in his ribs, or tossing and rolling about with drafts of cold air stabbing him here and there. Beds are important—and everything that goes to make beds sleep-producing. Important not only for comfort at night, but for comfort and joy throughout the day, for nothing wears one down quicker or jeopardizes his resistance more than inadequate sleep. The woods will soon turn dismal, the lake will lose its charm, the sunset its flame of beauty, and thoughts will turn to home and comfort.

The doctrine of "go light, young man" applies to bedding only with reservations for, while we would not want to haul one ounce of unnecessary luggage, here is one place where we will be well repaid in carrying everything essential to perfect comfort. Yet, curiously enough, it is right here that the average camper makes his greatest mistake—he hauls along useless gadgets no end yet skimps himself on sleeping facilities.

Camping originated in the need for a warm, comfortable place to cuddle up for the night, for it was when prehistoric man sought night shelter in the woods that the first camps came into being. And even the dog takes great pains to prepare his bed to suit him before settling down for the night. In fact every living creature does except that most absurd brand of tenderfoot who thinks that camping is roughing it.

Opinions differ as to what is best in the way of beds. If we are to sleep on the ground some sort of "mattress" is necessary. In camping on the same spot for some time, an elevated bed can sometimes be rigged up. Let us look at the devices for both of these possibilities.

BOUGH BEDS

The much glorified bed of balsam boughs is more satisfying to the nostrils than it is to the bones of hips and back. Its lovely, penetrating, woodsy perfume—the most fragrant thing in the woods—is a joy forever. But as a comfortable bed one would not rely upon it except with many tough portages ahead that required the elimination of every possible ounce of weight. If well made the bough bed is reasonably soft and springy, and it is better by far than sleeping on the bare ground even with hip holes dug to fit the body, but the time required to do a first-class job of one is so great as to argue loudly against relying on it as regular diet. Better to take a dependable camp bed along. However, the time will doubtless come sooner or later when we will have to make one of boughs or sleep on the ground, and so a wrinkle or two:

It is the twigs of *balsam fir* that have made the bough beds of the woods for these countless years and certainly their thick flat needles are unequaled for softness, but to get together enough of them for a good bed would be a two-hour task. Here is the wrinkle that will do it quickly: Mix balsam boughs with *spruce* boughs. The spruce boughs are longer and much springier but on the other hand are coarser and prone to poke one's ribs. To use them alone would not be desirable, but when mixed with balsam we have the perfect bed of boughs and one which can be made in a fraction of the time that balsam alone requires. As a substitute for balsam use *hemlock*, *juniper*, or *cedar*, but always over a foundation of spruce if possible.

First cut four logs, two of them five feet long and the other two seven feet, for a framework to prevent the boughs from scattering. Lay these on the ground in a rectangular shape and drive sticks on the outside so that they will not be shoved aside when you roll at night. Smooth up the ground carefully, removing all bumps and roots.

Now gather a couple of big armloads of spruce boughs of convenient size to be broken off with the hands. Starting at the top of the bed and pointing the tips towards the head, shingle the boughs over the entire bed surface in a rough sort of way without taking too much pains. Then gather a big armload of balsam boughs, perhaps the equivalent of a generous bushel-basketful, by grasping the twigs between the thumb and forefingers and snapping them downward—if too big to break in this way they are too large for use in the bed. These we must shingle over the spruce foundation very carefully. Starting at the head of the bed, set up the balsam twigs almost on end by shoving the butts down into the spruce boughs below, pointing the tips to the head always, and installing each succeeding layer so as to cover the butts of the previous one. It really makes little difference but the usual procedure is to place the under or silver sides of the boughs toward the earth—they are a little springier this way. Don't waste much time with the lower third of the bed for one's feet do not need a soft mattress anyway, but pile the boughs on generously beneath the hips and shoulders. In gathering the boughs do not take too many from any one tree.

If one is camping in a country where there are no evergreens, use *willow, cherry*, or any of the *broad-leaf* shrubs, but needless to say these are a poor second to the soft, downy balsam.

AIR MATTRESSES

Here is the camp bed without an equal unless we are on a trip where we must go extremely light. These luxurious, soft mattresses mean camping in complete comfort—and that is as it should be. True, they are a trifle heavy but the labor in hauling them is probably less than that required in making a balsam and spruce bed each night. If they can be hauled, then by all means take them for you will sleep in luxury.

The rubber mattresses can be inflated with the mouth but it is better to take along one of the small and very light pumps made for the purpose which can be rolled inside the mattress without adding materially to the bulk or weight. Particular care should be taken not to inflate the mattress too much because when fully blown up it becomes hard—judge it by lying on it, not sitting on it.

In cold weather do not depend on the mattress to keep you warm beneath but cover it with blankets. More than anything else it is dampness that chills and while the rubber mattress will keep out the ground dampness it does not permit the body moisture to escape, with the result that wool blankets should separate the body from the rubber.

Air mattresses are a little expensive, and while the confirmed camper will want them, the casual camper may find them out of his range. For these campers, the bedtick is the best substitute.

CANVAS BEDTICKS

Better by far than to rely on a bed of boughs in case you cannot carry a rubber air mattress, or do not care to invest the money in one, is to take along a canvas bedtick. One of these will roll up into a compact light little bundle, and if made of tanalite instead of canvas will weigh only a few ounces.

Made three feet wide and seven-and-one-half feet long the bag can be stuffed with grass, straw, or leaves to make a reasonably soft mattress when placed on the ground. But filling it is another of those jobs that takes much time.

Better to do it this way: Make the bag, as before, three by seven-and-one-half feet in size, but down each side of it run a row of

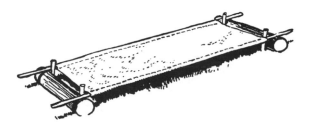

Figure 45. CANVAS BEDTICK UNFILLED

stitches three inches from the edge, thus creating an open hem on each side through which a pole can be run as in Figure 45. When the ends of these poles are placed over logs as in the illustration we have a comfortable enough bed just as it is, every bit as comfortable as a canvas cot. But we can turn it into a still more luxurious mattress by filling it with straw, grass or leaves, and then elevating it on the logs as before. A tick to be used directly on the ground should be waterproofed.

Often a single sheet of canvas is used in this way, the edges turned back and sewed to make the side pockets. But it is better to use the double sheet of canvas made into a bag so that it can be used either with poles as an elevated canvas cot or on the ground filled with straw.

The chief difficulty with stretched canvas as a bed is that it does not conform to the shape of the body. By substituting *burlap* or *coffee sacking* for the canvas in making the tick, a very much more comfortable bed will result when it is used unfilled, even though it may not be as substantial a one. The sacking will give and stretch with use until it sort of fits when one stretches out on it.

In pioneer days *beech leaves* were much used as filling for mattresses—they are springy and wiry, and make a comfortable tick. The leaves must be gathered before the frost hits them, however, for thereafter they lose their body. Gather the leaves and dry them before putting in the tick. This may take a little time but if one is going to camp on the same spot for some time it will be the means of producing a softer and more comfortable night's sleep than can be obtained by any other sort of stuffing readily picked up in the woods.

Indian Willow Bed

The modern camper used to his gadgets may label this as fanciful and fussy, the product of a romanticist's efforts to go primitive and play Indian. But it *is* a practical bed and the only portable one that is made in the truly woodcraft way of woodland materials, light and compact to carry, springy and comfortable to use, and costing little or nothing. It is the willow bed of the Plains Indians.

It was as a small boy that I first discovered this bed in visiting a boys' camp where Ernest Thompson Seton was a guest—he was lecturing in a nearby city and spending his nights at the camp. And he slept on one of these willow beds which he carried with him across the country. That was the inspiration and the beginning. I went home and made one, and I can still recall the happy, busy days, in the woods gathering the shoots, and in the attic assembling them. And the bed went with me on many and many a camping trip and hike to offer perfect rest while others tossed and cat-napped on the ground.

The making of these Indian beds just as the Blackfeet would do it is a rather lengthy task, calling for much patience, but my boyhood model was simpler and every bit as serviceable. Let us describe it first from my boyhood notes which I still possess, and then look into the authentic Indian way.

Hike to a nearby marsh, river or lake and cut seventy-five to one-hundred straight shoots of willow, kinnikinik, or arrowwood ranging in size from that of a lead pencil up to that of your little finger, together with three or four larger ones of thumb size. And in length they should produce straight sticks thirty-one inches long. Tie these very firmly into a bundle until they are ready to be used in order that they may remain straight and unwarped. A city substitute for willow shoots is found in doweling rods.

In addition a ball of strong cord, a spool of linen thread, and some beeswax are needed.

For a framework on which to build the bed, lay two short logs parallel to each other on the ground, six-and-one-half feet apart, and drive stakes either side to prevent them from rolling as in A, Figure 46.

Drive the four nails in each log as illustrated ten inches from each other, thus making the outer nails thirty inches apart. Cut four lengths of string each twenty feet long, double these and tie a knot at the loop end forming a three-inch loop as illustrated in B. Hook these loops over the nails on one of the logs as shown in A, and then twist rather tightly throughout the entire length, wrapping the other end around the corresponding nail in the other log. Now peel the willow shoots, trim each to exactly thirty-one inches, and cut a notch a half inch from each end. Select one of the larger shoots for the end rod. Separate the twisted strands of the string and shove the rod through as shown in A. At each intersection bind the rod to the string with a wrapping of well-waxed linen thread. Now insert the second rod about a half inch from the first and continue to install the rods in this way, alternating the butts and tips until the bed is six feet long. Terminate it at this point with another heavy rod.

Now we must make the tapered pillow shown in C, which is eighteen inches long and constructed by making the rods progressively shorter until the pillow is eighteen inches wide at the end. The ends of the string are then tied to form the three-inch loops as illustrated. In Indian fashion this tapered pillow end of the bed should now be covered with canvas used as a substitute for buckskin. And being the Indian bed that it is, the canvas should be ornamented with typical Indian designs.

To set up the bed for use, lay two four-inch poles on the ground parallel to each other and far enough apart so that the ends of the rods will rest safely on them, as shown in Figure 46. Drive pegs in

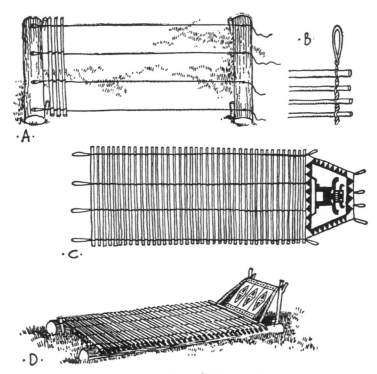

Figure 46. INDIAN WILLOW BED

the ground to catch the end loops and stretch the bed tight, and erect forked sticks to hold the pillow at the proper angle.

After a few nights of use the willow sticks will become bent and the bed will begin to sag. It is therefore desirable to turn the bed every few days and sleep on the other side.

When not in use the bed can be rolled into a compact bundle.

Authentic Indian Willow Bed.—Much more ornamental and elaborate was the authentic willow bed of the Blackfoot Indian, for time was never so precious to the old-time Redman that he felt justified in making an unartistic article of handicraft. Absolutely straight were the willow rods that went into his bed, whittled so that they were uniform in thickness throughout, and fully twice as many of them were incorporated in the bed as in the simple one just described, for they were placed so close together that they touched each other. The method of construction was also different: Two strings of rawhide thongs were stretched between the logs rather than four as in the case of the simple bed in Figure 46. Through the end of each rod a little hole was burnt with a hot wire, and through these holes a string was run and then doubled under the supporting cord below as sug-

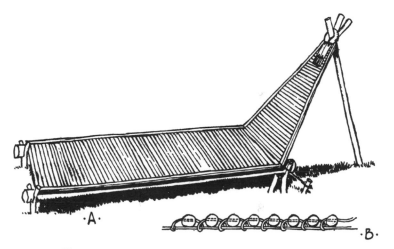

Figure 47. Blackfoot Willow Bed with Backrest

gested in Figure 47. The sticks all tied in place, a three-inch strip of leather colored red or blue or a strip of colored cloth was doubled over the edge and sewed, thus giving the bed an inch-and-a-half binding along the sides.

One of the most characteristic and ornamental features of the Blackfoot bed was the high back-rest at the head, and sometimes at both the head and the foot, as seen in Figure 47. The Indian would sleep on his bed at night and sit on it using the back-rest during the daytime. At the top of the back-rest is a heavy leather strap used as a hanger through which a pole was thrust and supported by a crotched stick, thus holding the back-rest upright. Elaborate beaded pieces were often draped down from this hanger.

The Blackfoot bed was either erected on logs in the same way as the simple bed we have described, or it was elevated on slender poles held aloft by crotched sticks as in the illustration.

ROPE BEDS

In rigging up a bed in a shack or an Adirondack lean-to, the usual procedure is to build a platform of boards on which to place the mattress. But no mattress that was ever purchased will make a board comfortable—the spinal column with its curve just wasn't made to rest on such a stretcher.

Better to make the bed out of rope if such is to be had in large enough quantities. Build a framework of poles, tie the rope to one of the side poles at the head end and then run it back and forth from one pole to the other throughout the length of the bed. Of course the strands of rope must be placed close together and a mattress of some sort installed above. If the rope is not drawn too unreasonably tight, one will nestle down on it and be at peace with the world. If too loose or too tight, a couple of minutes will adjust it while making the bed the next morning.

In pioneer days beds on this general order were made by tying withes crosswise of the bed frame.

Bed from Old Inner Tubes.—See Chapter XV.

SLEEPING BAGS

These are intriguing gadgets in many ways: One can drop his bag on the ground, crawl into it, and go to sleep—any place, any time. What about rain in the face?—there is usually a projecting canvas at the head end which can be rigged up with stakes so as to provide a little awning over the head. Mosquitoes? Well, you are supposed to take along some mosquito netting, spread it over your face, and pray that you won't roll over and toss it off.

There are arguments aplenty against the sleeping bag as an ideal bed in the woods. It is romantic in a way to drop one's bag down any place and crawl into it, sleeping very close to the fragrant earth and with the dashing rain striking the awning not more than an inch or two above your face. Before long, however, one gets a feeling of restraint, of being bundled up too much. And then, too, most sleeping bags do not take into consideration the fact that the temperature changes from night to night and even during the course of the same night. A bag put together for cold nights is much too warm on a warm night. Of course one can get into it with the blankets under him rather than over, but when the chill hours of the outdoor dawn come around, he will have to get out and crawl back in under the blankets, which is not strictly in line with most people's idea of comfort. It is easier and healthier to reach down to the foot of the blanket bed and pull up an extra cover. Again, if the sleeping bag is of the type with the blankets sewed in, it is very difficult to air and dry out, and this makes it a most unsanitary contraption. If it is of the type that uses separate or loose blankets, making it up each night is much more trouble than ordinary bed making. And lastly, one usually needs a tent or shelter of some sort anyway. True enough, he can sleep comfortably, provided there are no mosquitoes, with only the little awning over his head. But comes the rainy morning when he must pile out into the cold, wet woods and dress between spasms of shivering! Or comes the cold, *dry* morning, for that matter!

Better than a bag for adults is the little pocket-size tent, a mattress of some sort and plenty of good warm blankets. The only situation in which a bag proves more satisfactory than other beds is while camping in very cold weather, using it in connection with a tent. It has its advocates, however, much devoted to its use, and if you are given to joining this company, get a waterproof bag that permits the easy removal of the blankets for the daily drying out of the body moisture which accumulates in generous quantities while sleeping in a watertight bag.

These suggestions are made with the older boy and girl and the adult in mind. *For children the sleeping bag has the singular recommendation of holding the blankets in place,* eliminating all danger of their being tossed off. Without a sleeping bag blanket pins would have to be used to insure against exposure. For this reason they are favored in organized camps for use on trips and at out-camps.

BLANKETS

Did you ever reach for your cotton underwear or socks when you got up in the morning in camp only to find them cold, clammy and wet? It had not rained during the night and the clothing was in the tent, but it could not be more disagreeable had it been dropped into the lake. That is cotton's worst habit—it absorbs moisture easily and quickly but gives it up very reluctantly. And there is always moisture around camp, rain or no rain. The moral is to *stay away from cotton bedding*.

This means that quilts are to be avoided. They usually have a cotton covering and cotton padding of some sort inside. No one but the camper who has had experience with them in the woods can realize how thoroughly clammy and completely disagreeable a cotton quilt can be. Only the house-dweller can belittle this point. Even if there is no dampness without, the body gives off a surprising amount of moisture during the night which is absorbed by the cotton bedding with the result that we find ourselves sleeping cold in reasonably warm weather. And furthermore, the quilting compresses the padding within so much that no air space is left. The need is for loosely constructed covers containing plenty of air space to serve as insulation.

Comforters are much better than quilts and if filled with wool material rather than cotton, would be quite satisfactory were it not for their excessive bulk. Held together only at certain points, they are much more loosely constructed than quilts with their crosswise stitching. At best the comforter is a poor second to a wool blanket, however, but it does make a good undercovering if one does not have a thicker mattress of some sort.

About woolen blankets, there is one important thing to remember—*avoid closely woven blankets* and this means blankets of the army type. The army blankets are made to reduce bulk and are so tightly woven that they are about the coldest covering that one could ever hope to find. *The looser and fluffier the blanket the warmer it is.* That is why the Hudson's Bay blanket has been heralded throughout the years as the finest of blankets for the bush and probably so remains today. These blankets are not only fluffy and exceedingly warm, but are light in weight for their thickness, will not absorb moisture, and indeed will turn a reasonably heavy rain. They were originally made for the woods of the North and will stand rough usage. The warmest blankets are of llama wool and of camel's hair, but these are ruled out for ordinary camping because of their excessive expense.

Do not skimp on blankets—take a generous supply both for covering above and protection beneath. Remember that you need as many on one side of you as the other.

PACKS

The old adage that a camper is known by his fires contains much of truth, no doubt, but it is nearer the fact to say that he is known by his packs. The trail-wise old campaigner has all his duffel inside a sturdy pack that looks the part, hanging comfortably on his back or resting neatly in the bottom of his canoe, while the beginner shuffles along with an assortment of stuff sticking out in all directions from his back, belt, arms and hands. Just try to climb a hill or follow a trail through the brush with an assortment of loose articles in your arms! And having set up camp, the old-timer of the trails keeps his possessions inside his pack—he has a place for everything and keeps it there— while the tenderfoot has the ground littered with duffel conveniently exposed to the mice, squirrels and porcupines but where he himself cannot find it when he wants it. Not only for hauling but for housekeeping are packs essential. And inside the pack the small articles should be assembled according to type in smaller bags.

Yes, the camper is known by his packs but when it comes to what kind of pack to take there is no way to settle the matter once and for all for every kind of an expedition. There are many, many kinds of packs, each having admirers of its own who love to sing its praises. No space to discuss each of these, nor would there be any purpose—an outfitter's catalogue will do that. But a word is necessary as to suitable types:

SHOULDER STICKS FOR THE TRAMP

One can pack his belongings in a coffee-sack, stick it on the end of a pole, hoist the stick over his shoulder, and start on his merry way down the road—but he will look more like a tramp than a camper. That's good enough when sauntering down an open path to go fishing, but the camper has more than his lunch to pack.

BLANKET ROLLS FOR THE TENDERFOOT

Quickly to take on the guise of a tenderfoot, roll your blankets around your duffel into the traditional blanket roll, and sling it over one shoulder and across to the opposite hip. Blanket rolls are handy enough, and offer the most expedient arrangement for an overnight hike, but for longer than that they fall far short. It is a nuisance always to have your movements impeded by a roll across your chest, but the biggest shortcoming is that the roll offers no place to keep belongings when once in camp. If you hope to do much camping, better invest in a good back-pack.

RUCK-SACKS FOR THE HIKER

Only for the hiker or the mountain climber who wants to take a small amount of duffel with him is the ruck-sack recommended. The term ruck-sack is a German word meaning "back-sack" and the sack itself is of European origin, having been used these countless years across the European continent and perfected by long experimentation. There are many, many variations of the pattern, including the so-called Norweigian packs and certain types of haversacks. The characteristic feature of these light, small packs is that the shoulder-straps come together in a V in the middle of the back, thus causing the pack to hug the shoulders and placing the strain on the strongest part of the shoulders. With many pockets and designed for lightness, the ruck-sack is a convenient little rig for carrying the few items that one will need on a hiking trip. But it is not suitable for the camper who must haul blankets and provisions into the woods afoot or by paddle.

PACKS FOR THE CAMPER

Probably the most popular pack in the American woods is the Duluth or Northwestern. This is a large, sturdy pack that will haul one's blankets, duffel, and provisions for at least a week's stay in the woods, and is equipped with shoulder-straps and tumpline. The Duluth pack is wider and shorter than some other packs and while it is easier to find things in it than in the long, deep packs, it nevertheless is often a little too wide for a man with narrow shoulders.

There are many other packs on the general order of the Duluth, any one of which will answer the purpose of the bush traveler provided they are made of heavy, sturdy canvas and are thoroughly waterproof, equipped both with shoulder-straps and the tumpline. Among the Canadian campers there is a very popular pack on the order of the Duluth but a little longer and narrower which is called by some outfitters the Hudson's Bay pack.

In filling the pack the blankets should be folded to cover the entire backside of the pack, so as to form a sort of padding and prevent any hard items from poking you in the back. Nothing is more uncomfortable than to haul a heavy pack with sharp corners gouging in at every step. And there is no need for this if the blankets are properly spread.

Now in the Adirondacks and in fact in the northeastern area in general, the *pack basket* is the time-honored and respected means for hauling supplies on one's back. This is an ash basket built to fit the back and to carry by means of shoulder-straps. Viewed aside from any sentiment attached to it, about the only contribution it makes over a canvas pack is that, due to its rigid sides, one can haul canned goods, glass jars and similar hard objects in it with no fear that they will gouge his back, and can toss the pack down without danger of their being crushed or broken. On the other hand, the pack basket often proves cumbersome when it is empty or only partly filled, does not fit into a canoe as well, and is not as convenient to handle in a car, as is a canvas pack. And it is heavier.

These baskets must be obtained with a waterproof canvas covering if the duffel is to be kept dry, and this in itself weighs almost as much as a canvas pack. All large outfitters will supply these baskets and covers.

TUMPLINES

Not as a carrying device but as a safety measure is the tumpline important to the average camper.

The tumpline is a strap that fits over one's forehead so that the pack is carried by the neck muscles rather than those of the back. A pack-harness equipped with a tumpline only is definitely not to be recommended for a beginner or any average camper, but the back-pack which he should possess should have *both* shoulder-straps and tumpline. When the pack is being carried by the shoulder-straps the tumpline can be shoved over the top of the head for relief when the pack becomes heavy, thus dividing the load. But the chief contribution of the tumpline is a matter of safety: When one is walking across a stream on a fallen log, is climbing a steep hillside, or is otherwise in a precarious and dangerous situation in respect to footing, the *shoulder-strap should be slipped off and the pack carried by the tumpline only*. In case one falls the pack will then easily free itself. Many a catastrophe has resulted in the far woods when a camper has fallen into a stream with a heavy pack on his shoulders.

It is a byword of safety in the woods always to use the tumpline. and not the shoulder-straps if the footing is uncertain.

Duffel-Bags

The duffel-bag has enjoyed an unwarranted popularity because of its long use in camps for boys and girls, with the result that the average camper thinks in terms of a duffel-bag rather than a back-pack. This is unfortunate. A good, substantial back-pack is always more convenient to use than a duffel-bag, even though it is not to be carried on the back. The duffel-bag is to be recommended on a camping trip only to take care of the extras, the excess duffel which cannot be gotten into the back-pack. The duffel-bag can be placed across the shoulders on top of the back-pack where it will rest securely by force of gravity. To carry it alone would require a pack-harness with tumpline.

The old-fashioned duffel-bag which opens at one end is an abominable contraption because the article you want is sure to be stored at the bottom of it. By all means get one with a zipper opening down its side. Better not to get one at all but to use instead a back-pack. You will have to be traveling pretty heavy to be carrying more duffel than will go in the back-pack and thus necessitate use of an additional duffel-bag.

How Heavy a Pack?

A full-grown, strong and hardened man considers fifty to sixty pounds an ample load for his back if he must haul it for any length of time. *For adolescent boys* twenty-five pounds is considered right for safety and health. *For girls* no more than ten pounds should be undertaken.

None but the foolhardy pride themselves on the weight of the back-packs they can carry. Of course each of the types of individuals mentioned above can lift and haul packs heavier than the recommended weights but it is not wise for them to do so for any length of time. It's one thing to transport a pack over a portage of a quarter of a mile, another thing to pack for a couple of miles, and still another to haul it all day. Under each of these conditions the desirable weight would be different. But even for a short haul there is danger in the strain from an overheavy back-pack. It is better to make two trips than to risk injury.

DUFFEL

It all depends on where we are going and how we are going. If we must haul it all on our backs all the way then certainly we must go light indeed. If there are many portages ahead then we must cut the wangan down to where it is much lighter than would be necessary if we were to paddle all the way. And the picture changes again if we have a pack-mule to do the work. So there is no way to determine just what we should take for any and every kind of a trip.

Two things to remember—we are going to live comfortably in the woods and should take along every essential article for comfort; and secondly, we are not going to make a pack-horse out of ourselves and take one single unnecessary item. With these thoughts in mind and assuming that our tents, bedding and clothing are cared for, let us look over the items in the following list, weighing each in terms of our own needs:

Axes (see page 163)	First-aid kit
File for ax	Personal kit—pins, needles, thread,
Carborundum stone	buttons, etc.
Sheath knife	Camera
Pocketknife	Binoculars
Crooked knife	Compass
Tool Haft (assorted tiny tools)	Map-case
Pliers with wire-cutter	Whistle
Folding camp spade	Candles in metal box
Small roll of picture-wire or	Flashlight
square foot of rawhide	Waterproof matchbox
Glue in tube	1 yard cheesecloth (for meat)
Liquid solder in tube	Cooking outfit
Reel oil	Inspirator (see page 113)
Boot oil	Cooking gloves
Adhesive tape	Dishcloths
25' cotton rope	Reflecting baker
Ball of twine	Wire grill
Canoe repair outfit in small can	Waterproof food-bags
Fishing-tackle box	Ditty-bags

Adhesive Plaster—The Camper's Friend

The camper's pal is adhesive tape—and the bachelor's pal, too! And its use in first-aid is the least important of its contributions to the camper. It is a sewing kit, soldering kit, and general repair kit all in one. In a flash it mends almost anything. It is airtight and waterproof, and can be used on cloth, metal and wood.

If your trousers rip in camp just slap on a strip of adhesive tape and they are as good as ever. If your tent rips a piece of adhesive tape will make it as watertight as new. You can even mend a hole in a canoe with it so that it will do service. If a kettle or bucket springs a leak a patch of adhesive tape puts it in order again—when the tape comes off just put on another piece. A hot stone applied to the tape will serve to set it more tightly on wood and metal.

If your canoe paddle splits a little adhesive tape will mend it so that it will see you through the trip. Likewise if your ax handle splits a little adhesive tape wrapped around it will keep it functioning.

Have you ever had the lid come off a can of syrup in your food pack? Next time you will stick a strip of adhesive tape over the top of the lid and down onto the sides of the can to hold it on! If the condensed milk can is not emptied for breakfast, cover the hole with a patch of adhesive and it can be tossed about with safety. A strip of tape seals tight the lid of a baking-powder can, and likewise prevents the cork in a bottle from coming out.

If you want to seal a wooden box so as to make it airtight and watertight just cover the cracks around the lid with adhesive. And if the hinges come off the box, replace them with adhesive. You can even make hinges for a large packing box to be used as a camp cupboard with the tape (see page 195).

To repeat: *adhesive tape is handy stuff to have around.* Keep a little roll in the first-aid kit and leave it there for first-aid. And then buy a large supply to take along for general camp use—and there will be many uses for it.

Tools

One of the tiny tool hafts with an assortment of miniature tools enclosed in the handle will prove to be an extremely valuable thing to have along in camp and will save the necessity of taking several larger items—one of these so small that it can be held in the palm of the hand can be obtained at any hardware store. In lieu of this, the pocketknife should be of the Scout type with tools attached. A pair of pliers will find many unanticipated uses. A tiny role of picture-wire may prove valuable in an emergency and will also find use in suspending meat over the fire for barbecuing.

If a fishing-tackle box is taken along all of these tools can well be assembled in it, making of it a sort of miniature traveling hardware kit. This box is also the place for the oil, the liquid solder and the glue. Without a tackle box, this sort of duffel should be carried in a special ditty-bag.

If any item among the tools in the list might well be eliminated, it would be the folding camp spade or shovel, but if space permits it is a good item to have along for purposes of sanitation.

THE DITTY-BAG

Several of these small waterproof ditty-bags sold by camp outfitting companies are important in that they prevent small items from being scattered through the outfit. All small articles should be organized into piles as to type and placed in separate bags. At least three ditty-bags are essential, one for toilet articles, one for the personal kit containing tiny scissors, pins, needles, extra buttons, etc., including the ball of string, and the third for a first-aid kit unless a compact metal kit is used. Bags are less bundlesome than other types of containers.

The ditty-bag habit is an excellent one for the camper to get, for otherwise his duffel gets badly scattered and things cannot be found when needed. The experienced camper thinks in terms of bags for his various items. So, too, does the Woodland Indian of the trails, for in his pack one is sure to find many bags or at least cloth tied in the form of a bag around articles. The bags should be heavy, strong, and waterproof, for all duffel in camp takes much abuse.

MAP-CASES

Maps are an absolutely indispensable item when traveling in the woods, as important as the compass itself. And even if a group of boys or girls are going on a hike in semicivilized areas, a topographical map is a handy and interesting thing to have along. But maps will soon become crumpled from use, damp with perspiration when carried inside the shirt as they usually are, and water-spotted when used in a canoe. A carrying case is therefore important.

While these can be purchased from any camp outfitter, it is no trick to make one: Secure some transparent celluloid and cut two pieces eleven inches square. Place them together and double an inch-wide strip of adhesive tape over the edge, running it around three sides and leaving the fourth side open. Fold the map so as to show the areas being traveled and insert it between the celluloid from the open side. Thus the map is completely visible, yet protected from wear, rain, and splashing. It is of such size as to be carried inside the shirt if desired.

CAMP COOKING OUTFITS

The person who likes to camp and figures on camping often will want and should have an aluminum cooking outfit made especially for the trail, in which all the items needed for cooking and serving a meal nestle together and fit into a convenient carrying-case. These range in size from two-man outfits to those for a dozen people. The little one-man Scout outfit is not to be recommended unless one is going light and alone, because it does not offer adequate facilities for cooking a meal, the utensils being few in number and small in size—the two-man outfit is much to be preferred over two one-man outfits. Pots and pans of random size take up so much room that they cannot possibly be taken along on a camping trip, and to get together an outfit of sundry items that would nestle would be difficult and at best would result in a bulky and heavy collection.

The nestling aluminum outfits save much worry for there is no need to give a moment's thought to what to take along in planning a trip—everything is in the bag and we can just pick it up and go. The usual outfit contains kettles, coffee-pot, stewpan, skillet, breakfast-food bowls, plates, cups, salt and pepper shakers, and a kit of silverware, the side handles on all pots and pans being of the folding type. In this bag also would be carried the can-opener, matches, inspirator, and cooking gloves.

The silverware should be carried in a case of light cloth which in turn goes inside the outfit bag, in order to prevent the items from scattering and becoming bent.

The only items in an aluminum outfit that are undesirable are the cups. Aluminum cups are abominable things—the aluminum absorbs the heat of the coffee so that one cannot touch it to the lips, and when the aluminum is cool enough the coffee is cold. For these, substitute the stainless steel cups, which weigh but a trifle more, provided by outfitters.

For those who do not plan to take long trips into the woods but whose camping will be confined to occasional short expeditions, cooking outfits may be made from ordinary tin cans as described in Chapter XXIII. These quickly made tin-can utensils are serviceable and light, and a little planning will rig up a nestling outfit. They are much used by groups of boys and girls who like to camp and are often made in outdoor clubs and summer camps.

FOOD-BAGS

The average camper thinks of food-bags as essential only for the expert camper and explorer, but once one has had experience with these lightweight, paraffined containers, he will not care to go on a camping trip without them. Flour, sugar, and other materials affected by dampness can be placed in them and carried with complete safety. These bags come in an assortment of sizes from one pound up to ten or more pounds. Without them it is extremely difficult and indeed impossible to haul food on a camping trip and prevent it from scattering and getting wet. And there is no more disconcerting experience than to open the food pack and find everything messed up with scattered flour or sugar. The bags are so inexpensive that there is no need to deny oneself the convenience they offer.

CHAPTER VI

FIRE-CRAFT

THE SLOW SMOKE rises, and in it are hidden mysterious pictures that none but the children of the woods can see.... Food, warmth, protection—life itself—depend on precious fire. Cold, dismal, wet, the gloomy woods in one brief moment turn to coziness. Enough to hail a priceless gift, but more than creature comforts—mere animal needs—is found in this flickering magic! *There is spirit power:*

Within the circle of its light, camaraderie melts to friendship—close, sincere, fraught with deeper meaning than elsewhere in all the world. There is truth in the friendship symbol.

In its dancing flame, its glowing and fading embers, there are pictures—the food of imagination, the wine of creativity. Tonic for artist, poet, composer, inventor—for you and me—it is the charm of fertile fancy.

Alone beside the sacred fire, then it is that we hear the Voices, and the secret message of the Great One comes to us. So it was with the vigil Indian in yesteryears, so with the most practical in an external world today. In potent symbol fire transcends the mundane world.

So we court fire—for body, for spirit.

The Slow Smoke rises....

WHAT WOODS WILL BURN?

Most of the emphasis in fire-building instruction has been placed on the proper laying of the firewood, the arrangement of the sticks for various purposes. Many boys and girls can demonstrate several fire lays and recite rather glibly the good and bad points of each. Equipped with this training, it is surprising to find one of these campers kneeling over a fire carefully laid according to the correct formula, filling the air with explosives because it will not burn as scheduled! He has selected dry wood and cannot explain the failure. And in the meantime, dinner is delayed and everybody's temper is in an uproar.

This camper's woodcraft instructors apparently failed him on one most important point: he does not know one wood from another when it comes to burning and heating qualities. To him any solid, dry stick or branch is good firewood. This naïve assumption is responsible for more fire failures by far than the lack of knowledge of how to arrange the logs for this or that type of fire.

Since woods vary so tremendously in the way they burn, the heat they throw, and the cooking coals they produce, a familiarity with the trees that burn well is the most fundamental and important knowledge in fire-craft.

Of course, if one cannot recognize the different kinds of trees when he sees them, he cannot hope to be able to select good firewood for his cooking fires and campfires. There is of necessity, therefore, the closest correlation between fire-building instruction and nature instruction concerning trees. This fact has given many a camper the incentive he needed to learn the trees. For example, when a camper hears that hard maple is among the six best firewoods but that soft maple is relatively poor, he is going to want to know the difference in the appearance of the two kinds of maples. Or when he learns that the birches, particularly black and yellow, are among the best woods for all purposes, he has an excellent incentive to learn the birches. A compelling desire to learn the woodcraft of firebuilding opens the way in ideal fashion to the mastery of the nature-lore of tree familiarity.

And right here it should be said that it is important to be able to recognize the trees both from the leaves and the bark, for a solid dead tree of the firewood type has no leaves with which to publish its identity. But our task is to build the fires, leaving the tree instruction to the many excellent popular manuals dealing with them.

We must classify the firewoods in our minds into three types, for each has important uses: (1) *the short-lived woods* that burn with zest but are soon spent; (2) *the coal-producing* woods that burn slowly, evenly, and leave glowing heat in the coals long after the flame is gone; and (3) *the uninflammable woods*. There are still other woods that are of no earthly use whatever in fire building but these can scarcely be listed as a fourth class since they could not remotely be called firewood at all.

SHORT-LIVED SOFTWOODS

The gist of it is this: *Softwoods for a quick blast that is soon over, hardwoods for a steady, even fire with coals aplenty.* Exceptions, of course, as in every rule, but it's a safe formula as a general guide.

Of what use is the short-lived blast? Which leads to the second rule: *Softwoods for quick boiling and for baking, hardwoods for broiling, frying, and stewing.*

But let it be quickly understood that we are not using the term *softwoods* in the narrow, lumbering and forestry, sense as meaning the evergreens only, and hardwoods as meaning all other trees, but rather softwoods as meaning those species that have softer woods and hardwoods as those with harder woods.

The following softwoods will light easily and burn lustily but they just as quickly bog down to dead ashes. They are good kindling, good fuel for setting the kettle boiling in short order—this if your nerves will stand their crackling and spitting for most of these are among the spitfire woods. For sound and fury use:

Balsam
Spruce
White Pine
Pitch Pine
Alder
Basswood
White Cedar

Of these, *white pine* probably gives less heat than the rest although generous with flame and light, and quite often distresses with volumes of smoke. And *pitch pine*, although the richest of woods in the pitch within it, must be thoroughly dry—when green it refuses to do more than smolder. Similarly *chestnut*, high in moisture content when green, must be thoroughly seasoned. Of course it is assumed that all these woods will be used dry.

Better softwoods for burning are:

Jack Pine	Cottonwood
Buckeye	Quaking Aspen
Chestnut (well seasoned)	Red Cedar
Largetooth Aspen	Soft Maple

The *jack pine* of this list is an old standby in the northern pine country where good hardwoods are few and far between, much recommended by the trappers and guides of that area.

Tamarack is excellent and will be discussed below in connection with the lists of select woods. *Sycamore* is good but is tough to split which fact makes it uninteresting except when the bush offers nothing else that promises fire.

THE BEST FIREWOODS

Of course, beggars can't be choosers, and in practice it never is a question of the best firewoods the world produces, but rather the best the particular spot where we are camping has to offer. So let us first list the better woods for fuel, any of which would be excellent, and then evaluate them and compare them in selecting a few that can be called best.

These are good, lasting firewoods:

Apple	Maple, Sugar
Ash, White	Mulberry
Beech	Oak, White
Birch, Black	" Bur
" Yellow	" Chestnut
" White	" Live
Dogwood	" Overcup
Hickories	" Swamp Chestnut
Holly	" Swamp White
Hornbeam or Ironwood	Pine, Yellow
Locust	Tamarack

What do we mean by best in firewood? Woods that more than others will burn steadily, evenly, with constant heat, and leave glowing long-lived coals after the flame is gone! This means hardwood, for the softwoods let go with a blast of heat and just as promptly go dead; not necessarily the hardest woods, but the harder ones, for a few of those on the above list are but medium hard. The coal producing capacity of a wood is dependent upon its density and density is just another name for weight—hickory, a dense, heavy wood is famed for its coals but basswood, a light wood, yields its heat units quickly and is consumed in short order.

Viewed by this standard, what woods are best? Here they are:

Hickories	Black Birch	Beech
White Oak	Yellow Birch	Tamarack
White Ash	Sugar Maple	White Birch

Opinions differ as to which of these is the ideal fuel or as to the order in which they should be placed. Any one of them is certain to offer all that can be asked of firewood—it's only a question of which is nearest and handiest. Hickory is perfection itself, and if one of the woods must be placed above another, it would probably get the vote. But *sugar maple* and *beech* are of such excellence that they must be placed in the same class. And we must speak up for the *white oaks* too—no one could ask more of firewood.

Black and *yellow birch* are a woodsman's joy and there are many who class the birches as the ideal campfire wood, because they not only burn delightfully but are easy to ignite and quick to start, and the bark is the most prized of tinder for fire lighting. Of the birches, white birch is the poorest fuel, but it is still good and its bark is precious in wet weather.

Many campers have accustomed themselves to keeping their eyes alert for *white ash* while looking for a camp site, for it is not only excellent fuel but has the precious quality of burning almost as well when green as when dry, and withal it splits easily. For these reasons many call it the best all-around firewood.

There will be some who will question the presence of *tamarack* on the above register of the elite of firewoods. It is a conifer—the only one on the list. But my experience with it is that it has few superiors, if well seasoned—certainly it is better than white birch. It does not produce as generous a bed of coals as the others, but it burns with a steady, even heat that is ideal for the skillet, not too hot for the hands of the cook, and if well seasoned shows little or no annoying evidence of the usual spitting and crackling of the evergreens.

Necessity knows no law and if the immediate camp-site does not offer the best in wood we must content ourselves with what there is. In the evergreen sections of the north it is futile to long for hickory or other hardwoods that could be had in plenty in the hardwood belt farther south. There tamarack may be the best there is. But happily, the birches are also usually prevalent in the pine country.

As a general rule, the *red oaks*, those whose leaves have sharply pointed ends, are inferior as firewood to the *white oaks*. And the *elms* are relatively poor, slippery elm being better than white but still poor.

There are many woods that are quite uninflammable and utterly useless as fuel when green—these are listed later under "Uninflammable Woods." Their only service is as backlogs and andirons where they make an important contribution.

Mixing Woods for the Ideal Fire.—Remember the slogan, "softwoods for boiling, hardwoods for frying and broiling." A roaring flame is of no use for the skillet and will singe the hair of the cook who is handling it, yet flame helps to make the kettle boil. Kindling —softwood—is needed to get the fire started, so put the kettle on before the fire is lighted, thus using this first blast to set it simmering. But once it is boiling great heat is unnecessary because boiling water can't be made hotter than it is, no matter how much heat is put under it. The blaze started, put on the hickory, sugar maple, beech, or oak which will be burning steadily and evenly long after the soft "trash wood" is spent.

For a long fire, however, it is well to mix a little light wood such as buckeye, aspen, white pine or balsam in with the hardwood, particularly in the evening when the brighter flame will add increased cheer. Even in the cooking fire, a stick of softwood may be needed now and then to keep the hardwood from dying down. In all-night fires it is also well to mix in an occasional stick of light wood with the birch, beech or hickory that is used as the *pièce de résistance*.

GREEN WOODS FOR FUEL

Water will prevent almost anything from burning, and green wood possesses moisture. Common sense tells us, therefore, that green woods should not be relied upon for fuel unless dead woods cannot be located and that situation will very rarely if ever occur in the woods.

The only situation where green woods are used as fuel, except in dire necessity, is on a night fire where two or three pieces are added to a burning fire of dry wood. For this purpose the following woods will serve:

White Ash	Yellow Birch
Sugar Maple	White Oak
Beech	Soft Maple

Hickory

Of these, white ash is far and away the best burning green wood, having very low moisture content. All green fuel should be split quite finely.

The ease with which freshly cut green wood will burn depends largely on the moisture content. Green evergreens as a class possess much more moisture than do other trees and therefore offer no hope as fuel. The harder woods in general have less moisture. The moisture content of the outer layers, or the sapwood, is usually considerably greater than the inner layers or heartwood in both the hardwoods and softwoods. In green hardwoods, however, the difference in moisture content in sapwood and heartwood is much less than with softwood, and in some hardwood species heartwood has actually more moisture content than sapwood. Green *white ash* will burn quite readily, both the outside layers and the inner layers having very low moisture content. On the other hand, green cypress, having a moisture content of three to four times that of green white ash, could not be expected to burn.

Green woods will burn better if cut in the winter because they contain less sap at that season. And if possible they should be secured on high land because a tree cut there will have a much lower moisture content and will thus burn better than one of the same species cut on low land, in swamps, or on a river bank or lake shore.

Slow-Burning and Uninflammable Woods

For sidelogs on which to rest the kettles, for backlogs in the reflector fire, for andirons or fire-dogs!—indeed we often want to put wood in or near the fire for purposes other than burning. Among the woods that will not ignite, or which burn so slowly as to be considered uninflammable *when green*, are the following:

Ash, Black	Cypress	Pine, White
Balsam	Elder, Box	Sassafras
Basswood	Hemlock	Serviceberry
Buckeye	Maple, Red	Sycamore
Butternut	Oak, Red	Tamarack
Chestnut	" Water	Tulip
	Pine, Pitch	

Be it understood that these are to be used when green, for many of them will blaze avidly when dry. All of these will make dependable andirons and backlogs—in the pine and softwood country, pick up pitch pine, balsam, tamarack, or black ash, all green, of course, and if up on the higher hardwood levels, red maple, red oak, chestnut, or basswood will be handy.

CRACKLING AND SPLITTING WOODS

Like an endless string of little firecrackers with an occasional big one thrown in is the constant popping and banging of the spitfire woods. There is danger in them, too, for they spit their sparks across the lot to burn holes in the tent or blankets. There need be little fear, however, that the sparks of the spitting softwoods will set fire to the forest, except in an extreme drought, since they are not loaded as are hardwood sparks and do not smolder and burn long after lighting.

Here are the spitting and banging softwoods, some with greater proclivities than others in this respect:

White cedar	Balsam	Chestnut
Red cedar	Spruces	Tulip-tree
Alder	Soft Pines	Sassafras
Hemlock	Basswood	Willow
	Box Elder	

While not possessing the dynamite of the above softwoods, and of no annoyance to the ear, the following hardwoods sometimes toss sparks that contain a potential forest fire, holding their heat as they do and continuing to glow long after they light: *sugar maple, beech, hickory,* and *white oak.* Once the fire is well under way, however, these woods settle down and quit spitting, and so need watching only at the start. *Soft maple* also does a little spitting and barking, louder but less dangerous than the hardwoods named, but not so violent as the woods on the crackling list.

The cause of crackling and spark throwing is not well understood. Two factors that are probably involved are density of the wood and moisture content. For example, willow, a notoriously noisy wood, is a very light wood, whereas oak, a silent wood tossing very few sparks when well seasoned, is heavy. A glance at the spitting list will reveal that they are all light woods. The heavy woods throw an occasional spark but only when first lighted, that is, before the heat has dried out any moisture they contain.

Natural Tinders and Kindling

The answer is easy—*birch-bark*. The one and only tinder if it is to be had, so vastly superior is it! But sometimes it is not at hand and we must go a-foraging for others. Here they are, each of which will be expounded—*pitch wood, twigs, other barks,* and *fuzz-sticks.*

Birch-Bark.—One of the most inflammable things in the woods— rich and resinous—birch-bark ignites with the touch of a match, burns furiously with lusty flame and much heat, and endures long enough to set any well-laid fire ablaze. It is the torch of the Indian, the friend of all woodsmen. A little sliver of it is sufficient to light wet twigs. It is affected not at all by rain—I have submerged a bit of it in water for half an hour, taken it out dripping wet, and set it ablaze at the first touch of the match! It does its own "blowing" from the oil within it, reminding one of an energetic blowtorch.

The bark of any of the birches will do—white, yellow, black, red— but white birch is usually used if handy. A tiny strip is all that is needed, *so there is no need to strip a tree to secure it:* Small coils work themselves loose from the tree and fall to the ground normally, and since the bark is almost decay-proof a few minutes search in birch country will usually reveal a quantity of it on the ground. Or one of the loose coils can be pulled from a tree without leaving a mar of any kind. Never strip solid bark from a live tree for tinder—it is unnecessary and isn't done except by that type of vandal known as bark-peelers.

I usually carry a coil of birch-bark in my pack against the rainy day when tinder will not be handy. A dead log will produce enough for a whole camping trip.

Pitch Wood.—Fat pine is kindling without a superior. A chip the size of your hand will burn dramatically for better than fifteen minutes. The only reason why birch-bark is labeled as superior is because it is usually easier to get—it can be picked up, whereas a little chopping is necessary to get the pine chips. But so precious is fat pine that when a stump is discovered a quantity of little chips should be chopped loose and a ditty-bag filled with them and carried along as part of the pack outfit.

Old stumps are the best source of fat pine, especially if the tree died standing, for the pitch settles into the stump, hardens, and there remains; and being almost decay-proof the stump endures for many, many years. A dead stump may be decayed down to the level of the ground but the chips of it will still be rich in pitch, or the core of a dead stump the outer layers of which are crumbling away will doubtless be solid with the precious resin. All such stumps split very easily. Stumps of *white pine, Norway or red pine, pitch pine, balsam or spruce* are excellent. Of course, there is no way to tell what kind of wood an old decayed stump is, but if it is very old in the evergreen country and still keeping its shape, the chances are it has resin in it, and a chip pried loose will tell the story for if the brown, gummy pitch cannot be seen, a touch of a match will settle the matter. The Indians tell me that the very old and big pitch stumps are Norway pine, saying that this wood is richer in resin and more resistant to decay than white pine.

Another source of pitch is *pine knots,* pulled loose from a dead and decayed pine log. The knots are the butts of branches and, being filled with resin, will be found sound and good in a punky old trunk. Often they can be pulled out with the hands, or a tap of a stick will loosen them. The ax should be kept away from a knot itself; if it is necessary to chop it out, cut wide and deep around it. *Balsam* and spruce knots are also excellent but stay far away from *hemlock* if you have any respect for your ax, since these knots are as hard as granite and of no more use as tinder.

Other Barks and Cones.—*Cedar bark* is good tinder for starting a fire—it scales loose from the tree and a handful can be easily pulled off.

One of the most precious materials for fire-craft in the woods is *hemlock bark.* While scarcely a tinder in that it requires a starting flame, it burns readily and produces hot, glowing coals in no time at all. There is no way to produce coals for cooking so quickly—five minutes will produce more coals than a half hour of burning a hardwood fire. A fire of softwood to get the kettle simmering, followed by a generous quantity of hemlock bark for coals is the quickest way to cook a meal. In fact *most hardwood barks* will burn well and produce coals.

Dry *evergreen cones* are very inflammable and fairly explode with flame and heat when put on the fire. A tiny flame from a scrap of birch-bark and a few pine cones on top will set the hardwood going in short order. Often a little blast of heat is necessary to finish a meal and for this pine cones are made to order.

Twigs.—Not always are we in the pine and birch country with its rich, resin-filled tinder and are forced to fall back onto twigs, which is no hardship if two simple rules are followed: *First,* keep the twigs small, from the size of a straw up to half the size of a pencil—you can't light a log by touching a match to it. Twigs no thicker than a match can be found in abundance. *And second,* never rely on twigs that are in contact with the ground—the floor of the forest is always covered with a layer of tiny twigs, but these are certain to be damp except in periods of extreme drought, and even then contain more moisture than one might think. Rather, break them off snap-dry from standing trees near the ground, or, if ground wood is used, from the tips of branches extending up in the air—such twigs will be dry when all else is damp. In using stuff this small there is no need to worry about the kind of wood. In the autumn a few dry weed stocks may be mixed with the twigs.

A good handful is needed. Lay them parallel to each other and break off the ends so that they are about uniform in length, forming a bundle about a foot long. Grasp the bundle in both hands and snap the twigs in the middle, being careful not to sever them completely so that they can be set up on the ground in the form of a pyramid as in F, Figure 48. Lay slightly larger twigs against them and then add split kindling in the form of a wigwam.

Remember to keep it small—the whole wigwam, kindling and all, should not be over a foot in height. *And remember* that fire burns upward so keep the wigwam tall and slender. *Don't pack the sticks too close together* because fire needs air. So arranged, a match to the pyramid of tiny twigs in the center will set it ablaze.

Fuzz-Sticks.—Fuzz-sticks are items made without end in college camping courses, institutes, and organized camps, but curiously enough are rarely employed in the woods. For they are seldom necessary and always take time. The bountiful forest offers too much easily ignited tinder, to be had for the taking, to justify a fuzz-stick at any time except in a wet-weather emergency. The principle of the fuzz-stick is sound and a well-made one is a sample of good craftsmanship, but the objective is to produce a fire in the shortest possible time rather than to display one's whittling ability. Only in parks and semi-

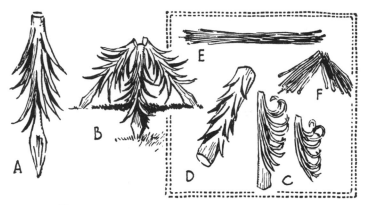

Figure 48. Tinder for Lighting the Campfire

civilized areas where conditions are admittedly different than in the wilds would a fuzz-stick be needed under normal conditions.

But to know how to make one is nevertheless important: Secure a stick of dry softwood a foot long and an inch thick. Point the end as in A, Figure 48 and, holding it by the pointed end, place the other end against a log or tree trunk and whittle long slender shavings, leaving them attached to the stick as illustrated. To prevent the shavings from being cut loose, press harder and deeper with the knife as the end of the cut is neared. Stick the fuzz-stick in the ground by the pointed end and stack the kindling over it. Or, in more typical institute fashion, make *three* fuzz-sticks and arrange them in a tripod as in B, Figure 48 as a foundation for the kindling.

Quicker and more bush-like than taking the time to make fuzz-sticks is merely to use fuzzed-up sticks. Whittle a few long shav-

ings from a split stick leaving them attached at one end as in C,
Figure 48, and then quickly rough up the edges of a few sticks of
kindling with the knife as in D, producing attached shavings or fuzz
an inch or so long, laying these wigwam-fashion over the little pile of
shavings. Fuzzed sticks light more readily than otherwise in rainy
weather. This can be done in a fraction of the time required for the
complete textbook fuzz-stick.

Kindling.—Any of the free-burning, short-lived softwoods make
good kindling—*cedar, balsam, basswood, pine, spruce, quaking aspen.*
They will contribute little to the fire other than as kindling and should
be relied upon only to get the hardwoods burning. *Remember that
split wood burns much more readily than round sticks.*

Artificial Tinders

In every camping outfit there should be an emergency kit of tinder
against that rainy day when all the world is drenched in water and
natural tinders capable of burning in the wet are not in sight. The naïve
confidence that a fire can always be built somehow is born of inexperience. The very situation that prevents fire making is the very one that
demands an immediate fire. *An emeregncy tinder kit is good woodcraft.*

A little roll of birch-bark in the pack is excellent fire insurance, and
should be carried, but most experienced campers prefer to take even
greater precautions in the form of artificial tinders:

Trench Candles.—These are the most practical and foolproof of
emergency tinders—and of emergency lights for the tent, too. They
are easy to make, easy to light, and burn for several minutes in the
rain. A few of them protected in a tin can with a top that screws on
will mean that we shall never be without fire, no matter how drenched
the forests may be. But they should be regarded strictly as an emergency resort and carefully guarded, awaiting that day when all else
fails.

To make them, roll up newspapers in fairly compact rolls an inch
in thickness and tie with a string. Then cut up into four-inch sections,
tying each section. Melt paraffin in a kettle and drop the newspaper
wads into it until thoroughly soaked, then remove and let harden.
When a match is touched to one of these it lights immediately and,
once the campfire is going, the candle can be extinguished and saved.

Purchased Tinder Kits.—The larger camp outfitters provide little
kits containing chemical tinders for emergency use, all inexpensive

and all guaranteed to burn in the rain. These are made expressly for the inevitable rainy day that sooner or later comes in every camper's life.

FINDING WOOD IN THE RAIN

It depends on where you are. If there is fat pine about, just go ahead and build the fire with it—no cloudburst will put a damper on its ardor to burn. If there is birch-bark handy, use quantities of it under the driest wood to be had and its hot blaze will soon rout the dampness. If you have an emergency kit of artificial tinder in your pack the problem is solved, whether or not there are natural tinders at hand. If dead sassafras twigs are handy, they will offer greater promise of burning than most other twigs that could be secured in the wet.

Without these, our ingenuity must come into play. If there is a small dead cedar, balsam or spruce about, drop it and split it up—the dampness from the rain will be only skin deep and the wood will split dry. Whittle off some shavings, fuzz up the sticks with your knife, and light. A large dead softwood, too big to drop, will usually have one dry side, and if not, the wet area is sure to be shallow, so chop into it and split off the sticks needed. Or try the underside of a large fallen log. It gets down to splitting the inner wood from some sort of tree, either standing or down.

Build the fire under a big log, below a leaning tree, under a projecting rock, or somehow protect it as much as possible from the rain. A good plan is to erect the crane for the pots first and then drape your poncho over it into a sort of pup-tent to shelter the fire until it is going. And it is important to protect the wood while splitting it and carrying it to the fire—there is little point in chopping for dry wood and then allowing the rain to wet it.

In the wet *the wigwam fire is the best* because it is tall and slender, the sticks so arranged that only the ends touch the ground. It should not be built directly on the ground, but rather placed on stones, bark or a layer of brush. Tinder also should be elevated from the ground and the fuzz-stick, if used, should not be stuck into the wet earth.

In dry and calm weather the usual way is to build up the fire before lighting it, but *in rain and wind the procedure should be reversed.* Have the kindling handy, light the shavings and then start feeding the blaze. It is easier to coax the flame if unhampered by sticks above it.

FIRE FUNDAMENTALS

There are two fundamental fires—the *wigwam* and the *crisscross*. Each is an essential fire in its own right, and each is a basic element in practically all other fires, whether cooking fires or campfires. These two every camper should know thoroughly as elementary fire-craft.

But first off, a few fire principles:

1. *Split wood burns better than unsplit wood.*

Don't turn your nose up at squaw wood—every woodsman uses it —but if it is larger than two inches in diameter, you will save time by splitting it. Why?

2. *Fire needs air.*

Don't pack the wood too tightly—leave plenty of air space. A loosely laid fire gains momentum fast while a compact one struggles and gasps for air.

3. *Draft makes the fire burn.*

Arrange the fire so that the wind can get at it. And beware of counterdrafts—two drafts fight each other.

4. *Flames rise upward.*

Make the fire tall and slender—let the flames run up the sticks. A low fire is a listless one.

5. *A fast-burning fire is soon spent.*

Some woods give up their heat units quickly—these go dead just as quickly. Slow-burning woods cook the meal.

6. *Flames for boiling and baking, coals for broiling and frying.*

Boil the kettle while the kindling is flaming; use the skillet when the coals appear.

7. *Softwoods for flame and a quick blast, hardwoods for coals and steady heat.*

A good fire needs a little of both.

8. *Keep the fire small.*

Big fires mean work—and why work? Anyway, no one likes to cook over a blast furnace.

9. *Put the kettle on before you light the fire.*

It's the flame that makes the kettle boil and it's the kindling that flames. Conserve the heat of the first blast.

10. *Have all the wood ready before the fire is touched off.*

To go wood hunting after the blaze is started is to throw away heat.

11. *Don't do one stroke of unnecessary work in building the fire.*

Textbook fires show every stick cut to uniform length—actual backwoods fires are rough and irregular, made from what is handy. Why chop a log if it can be burned in two? Good camp housekeeping means cleanliness and clear grounds, but does not demand that every fire be a show piece. If the fire does its duty, that is enough. There are too many uses for one's energy in the woods.

12. *Every fire should be planned before it is laid.*

The plan depends on what you are going to cook. Without the right fire the meal may be a failure. There are many plans in the pages following.

And a safety principle or two:

1. *Fire should be built within ten feet of the water's edge.*

That is a hard and fast rule in the canoeing country of the north.

2. *If it must be in the woods, it should be built on solid earth.*

The forest floor is inflammable often to a depth of two feet. Try digging to put out a fire that has got out of control in the woods!

3. *Saturate the fire with water before leaving.*

And then put some more water on it. Dig up the ashes with a stick to let the water down.

4. *Smothering a fire with earth is often dangerous.*

Fire often smolders underground for many days, eventually to flame forth again. Only on solid ground is it safe.

THE WIGWAM FIRE

Every novice knows the wigwam fire—indeed if a child who has never made a fire were told to build one, he would surely turn up with a wigwam, for it is the natural arrangement. But nevertheless it is not without importance in the craft, for it is the core of every fire lay no matter how elaborate. Viewed in its own right and aside from its contribution as the starting torch of other lays, it has few qualifications as a cooking fire if one intends to do more than stew a pot of tea, because its heat is all thrown to the center of the pyramid and offers no spread for the utensils, and its coals all drop to one small spot in the center. It is good for light, however, and is prized in the evening.

First the coil of birch-bark, or the chip of fat pine, or the handful of tiny twigs broken into a pyramid, or the fuzz-stick; then a few softwood sticks from the size of a pencil up to that of your little finger, stacked around it in wigwam fashion, and lastly the hard-wood sticks of finger and thumb size. Leave a little opening for the match to reach the tinder. Remember to keep it tall and slender. And

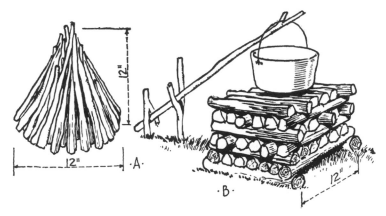

Figure 49. THE WIGWAM AND THE CRISSCROSS FIRES

keep it small—a foot high and a foot wide at the base—as seen in A, Figure 49.

CRISSCROSS FIRE

This is a fire of first importance—a fundamental fire used in many other lays and an unexcelled fire in itself. No arrangement of wood will burn so effectively, for none admits so much air to every stick and from all directions. And no other fire will burn down to a uni-formly spread bed of coals in so short a time.

First place the tinder—birch-bark, fuzz-stick, etc.—on the ground and build a tiny wigwam fire above it not over six inches high. Now place four base poles, each two inches thick and a foot long, around it, the corners overlapping log-cabin style, as in B, Figure 49. Over this lower course, stack up finger-and-thumb-size sticks of hardwood in crisscross fashion bringing the structure up to ten or twelve inches in height, as in the drawing.

Hang the kettle over it before you touch it off for this lay burns with a blast and will have the water boiling pronto. When it falls to coals flip out any smoldering butts and pull in the two upper base poles far enough to furnish a support to the skillet. It can't fail to cook a good meal quickly if the wood is right.

In rain or strong wind it is better to get the kindling going and the little wigwam well ablaze before the sticks are stacked on criss-cross. Laying up the complete fire before lighting conserves heat but lighting is hard to do in rain, and to attempt it may necessitate tearing down and starting over if the fire fails to catch.

THE INSPIRATOR

This precious device for inspiring a fire to burn was invented by Stewart Edward White, and as a cure for balky campfires is without equal. Secure about eighteen inches of rubber tubing of the size of your little finger from the drug store and slip onto one end of it a four-inch metal tube of about the same thickness. Just hold the metal end down to the fire and blow in the other end! The result is a veritable bellows that will blow up into a lusty flame the most stubborn of fires. After the tinder is lighted a puff or two will set all ablaze, and when the flame becomes listless a few blows will give it energy anew. As compared to blowing with the mouth or fanning with the hat, the salient advantage of the inspirator is that it localizes the draft to the exact point where it is needed—the metal tube can be inserted under the wood if need be.

Coiled up inside one of the kettles to take no room, the inspirator has been a regular, essential and indispensable item in my cooking outfit these many years.

In more truly woodcraft fashion, an inspirator can be made from a stick of *sumac* or *elderberry*. Run a hot wire through the center to clean out the large pithy center and create the hole, clean off the bark and whittle down to a convenient hollow tube. A stick a foot long is large enough to keep the face away from the heat and not too large to fit nicely into the cooking outfit.

TYPES OF COOKING FIRES

It all simmers down to three. Many and sundry are the possible fires, as many as there are campers in the woods, for every woodsman has a favorite type whose praises he loves to sing. In this maze of "best" fires one gets lost and bewildered, but an analysis of them shows that they are all variants of three lays, and for all practical purposes, of one. Knowing these, together with the two fundamental fires already described, we are equipped: (1) *the hunter-trapper type*, (2) *the reflector type*, and (3) *the underground type*. And the functions of all three can really be performed by the hunter-trapper type and its modifications. There are several variants of each depending on the available wood, but these anyone will figure out for himself if he knows the type. However, we shall describe the characteristic fire of each type, and then its more useful offshoots.

Hunter-Trapper Fires

This is the all-around cooking fire without an equal. It has been so regarded since first the pioneer stepped foot on the American continent, and it is still the favorite today. Save for one thing—it takes wood aplenty, and in some places wood is becoming increasingly scarce. But there are variants and modifications for such a scarcity.

Figure 50. Hunter-trapper Fire

Here is the Number 1 fire—ideal for all-around use. Equipped with a thorough knowledge of it and its offspring, no other fire will really be needed. First the authentic pattern, then the variants:

The True Hunter-Trapper.—Its characteristic is two side-logs on which the cooking utensils are supported, laid either parallel or at a slight angle, and of such distances apart as to accommodate the pots and pans—if at an angle the narrow end is for the smaller pots. If it's a camp for several days, the side logs should be of uninflammable wood (see page 102), otherwise any green wood. Logs six to eight inches in width and four feet long are right.

Place the logs so that the wide end is at a slight angle to the wind, as shown in Figure 50. Note the damper stick, a green billet placed under the end of one of the logs when the fire is being lighted and withdrawn when it is going, to be replaced only when fuel is added or more heat desired.

Put the tinder between the logs, a few small softwood sticks above in a little wigwam, and then build a crisscross on top the side-logs as

Figure 51. STONE HUNTER-TRAPPER FIRE

follows: put short sticks across the logs, long sticks lengthwise over the opening, more short crosswise sticks, more long lengthwise sticks, etc. Set fire to it and it will soon drop to the ground between the logs. As added fuel is needed long sticks are laid lengthwise between the side-logs. The fire must be long enough to accommodate three or four pots and kettles set in a row on top the side-logs, hence the long crisscross arrangement.

What are the advantages of the hunter-trapper? The side-logs confine the heat without exposing it to all outdoors, radiating it upward onto the utensils, and at the same time offer support for the pots without the trouble of erecting a lug-pole or crane.

Stone Hunter-Trapper Fire.—When wood is scarce and side-logs are not to be found or it is not wise to burn them, stones may be substituted—a row of large stones along each side, or many small ones built up to a height of five or six inches, as in Figure 51. A large stone may close one end if desired, turning it into a three-sided fireplace. Build the fire within as in the regular hunter-trapper. Avoid water-saturated limestone—*it pops.*

As a rule stones provide a rather tipsy support for pots and pans and so are a second choice to logs. It is usually necessary to hang the kettles by pothooks from a crane (see page 145) rather than trust the irregular stones.

In case one only has a quick lunch to prepare there would be no need to set up the complete hunter-trapper arrangement—three stones arranged as in Figure 52, with a wigwam fire built around and in the spaces between them will hold the skillet or pot.

The Trench Fire.—This variant of the hunter-trapper type is the most economical of fuel and the safest. Long popular in wood-scarce Europe, it has never been extensively used in its true form in the American bush where wood is to be had in abundance. It is always easier to build a fire on top of the ground than to dig a pit for it. But once the trench has been completed the tending of the fire becomes a simpler task because the same amount of wood lasts longer. Necessity is fast shoving it to the fore in certain areas in this country, particularly in supervised regions such as reserves and parks where authorities insist on it for safety and economy.

Figure 52. THREE-STONE FIRE FOR A QUICK LUNCH

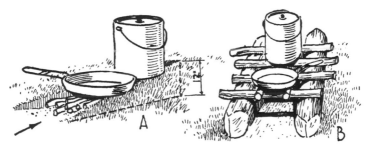

Figure 53. THE TRENCH FIRE AND THE TRENCH HUNTER-TRAPPER

Although it is really a fire in the ground and could be classed under that heading in the section following, it is nevertheless an obvious variant of the hunter-trapper, sunk in the ground instead of edged by side-logs, and so designed that the kettles rest on the edges of the trench.

Dig a trench four feet long, larger if there are many kettles, sloping it gradually from the surface to a depth of one foot at the far end. The deep end should be a little less than the width of the smallest kettle and the trench should gradually widen to twice that width at the shallow end, as shown in A, Figure 53. The walls should be perpendicular and, if the earth is so soft as not to support the pans, should be lined with rock. *The wide end should face the wind.*

Put a goodly supply of tinder under a little wigwam fire and stack up the crisscross fire over it on the ground surface, using long and short sticks in the arrangement described for the hunter-trapper. Squaw sticks of hardwood are good enough to reinforce the blaze because very little fuel is needed in a fire in the ground These trench fires are appreciated on a hot day.

Trench Hunter-Trapper Fire.—This is an ideal combination of the trench and the true hunter-trapper, of excellent breeding in the American woods and long associated with more permanent camps in the bush. Delightfully combining the qualities of both fires, it is a cool fire for the cook in hot weather, conserves heat, and is at once handy for boiling, frying, and baking.

Build the trench fire just as described, and then place the two six-inch side-logs along its edges as in the usual hunter-trapper. Then lay two or more small green poles across the side-logs to serve as andirons on which the kettles are to rest, as shown in B, Figure 53, these being necessary because the side-logs will be a little too far apart.

Boil the kettles when the fire is first lighted, rake the coals to the shallow end for frying and boiling, and then place the pan for baking on the hot ground in the deep end. Two large logs may be placed crosswise when the fire is first lighted, setting their undersides aglow with coals, and then placed across the deep end above the baking-pan to supply additional heat, *but beware of too hot an oven!*

The Backlog Fire.—Another variant of the versatile hunter-trapper of good vintage, calls for one large log as seen in Figure 54. The hunter-trapper may be quickly turned into this type as occasion demands by removing one side-log and using the other as the back-log. Out from the backlog place two uninflammable firedogs, measuring about three inches in thickness, and across these lay uninflammable cross-sticks as needed to support the pans. This arrangement necessitates a pot-hanger leaned against the backlog with its butt stuck in the ground.

Build the fire in the usual crisscross fashion in front of the backlog and utilize the flame to boil the kettle. Then rake the coals forward under the pans, adding more fuel to blaze under the kettle. This is

Figure 54. THE BACKLOG FIRE

the advantage of the backlog fire—*both coals and flame can be had at the same time.*

FIRES BELOW GROUND LEVEL

Two times they are appreciated—on a hot day, when the cook finds relief in the scant heat they throw into his face, and when wood is scarce for they do much with little, and squaw wood is as good as any in them. Cooking in a hole is a good habit to get.

The trench fire already expounded is of this kind, although classified in this chapter as a variant of the hunter-trapper. And there are others:

Hole Fire.—This is for a small, quick meal: Excavate a hole a foot wide and eight inches deep, *piling the dirt on the side away from the wind,* as in Figure 55. Fill with tinder, build a crisscross lay of small hardwood above it, and set fire. When it

Figure 55. FIRE IN A HOLE FOR A QUICK LUNCH

falls, flip out the smoking butts, put two green cross-sticks across it for the skillet, and cook in comfort. If there is a kettle, it is suspended on a pot-hanger before the fire is touched off.

This is a good hike or picnic fire for steak on a stick, kabobs, wieners, and the like—the meat sticks may be laid on the ground extending over the coals, and will cook unattended.

Automatic-Stew Fire.—Stew requires a slow, steady, and long fire—that's why a fire in a hole is good. A hole prepared as in the preceding fire, with the stew kettle above the crisscross before it is lighted, and then lowered very close to the coals after it has fallen in the hole, makes an ideal stew fire—a little fuel can be added from time to time as needed.

But if you want to go fishing for an hour, set up a row of hardwood sticks around the edge of the hole as in Figure 56. Automatically these sticks will fall as the bottoms burn away and the stew will continue to simmer away.

Here are the requirements: a hole with perpendicular sides large

Figure 56. FIRE IN A HOLE FOR STEWING

enough so that there will be a space of four to five inches all around and below the kettle when hung well down in it as in Figure 56; slow-burning hardwood sticks—sugar maple, white oak, hickory, beech, yellow birch, sycamore, persimmon. Green and dry sticks should be mixed for best results.

The automatic feature of a stew fire in a hole is a novelty that will seldom find use because the conditions calling for it are remote to most campers, but it will function if intelligently handled.

Fires for Cooking Underground—The Bean Hole and the Imu.—Food may be cooked underground either in pots or without utensils.

Bean-hole beans and similar dishes are of course cooked in a kettle with a tight cover. The imu uses no utensils.

The heat for cooking underground in a kettle is provided by coals. Dig a hole a foot deeper and a foot wider than the pot. Fill generously with tinder and small sticks, and over the top erect a large crisscross fire, using the best of hardwoods—hickory, beech, sugar maple, white ash or yellow birch—for we must have coals and more coals. Here is a case where the make-it-small rule of fire building does not hold—make it big and use wood unstintingly. When it falls to coals in the hole, shovel out all but a thin layer across the bottom, put in the tightly covered bean pot which has been heated over the fire, shovel the ashes back in the hole, packing them around the sides and over the top of the pot. Cover the hole with dirt packed tightly and build the evening campfire over the spot. Dig up the beans for lunch or dinner the next day and they will be deliciously done provided you put enough water in the pot to completely cover them before sealing—otherwise they may be dry.

For cooking underground without a kettle, hot stones are needed rather than coals. The imu hole will negotiate successfully chicken, fish, meats, corn on the cob, potatoes and other large vegetables. Dig a hole fifteen to eighteen inches in diameter, depending on the quality of food. Lay the crisscross fire over the top as usual but intersperse the layers of wood with stones the size of your fist—there must be stones enough completely to line the bottom and sides of the hole. Avoid water-saturated limestone which explodes when hot. Use lots of wood, good hardwood, and get the stones as hot as possible. When the fire collapses, shovel out the coals, spread the hot stones over the bottom and sides, throw in several large handfuls of vegetable tops or leaves from broad-leaf trees, place the food on the leaves, cover with several handfuls more of leaves, and spread a wet burlap over. Now set a stick up in the middle of the pit, and fill the hole with dirt packing tightly around the stick. Very carefully remove the stick, pour a gallon of water down the hole and quickly fill the hole with earth—the water is necessary to provide the steam for the cooking.

In selecting the leaves avoid nut-bearing trees, aspen, and poplar. They are bitter.

In two hours the food should be ready for the big moment of opening the hole.

If a large quantity of food is to be cooked, a piece of chicken wire or better still gravel screening will help much in withdrawing the food from the hole: after the bottom layer of leaves is in place, put the food on the wire, lower into the hole, and then cover and fill as before. In withdrawing the food, merely pick up the edges of the wire and lift it out. If it is a big imu, garden rakes will be helpful in lifting the wire screening—just hook them into the edge of the wire.

REFLECTING AND BAKING FIRES

Only if one intends to bake biscuits or bread, or roast his meat, will reflecting fires become essential or important. There are two main types—the hunter-trapper variants and the reflector fire.

Figure 57. REFLECTING FIRES FOR BAKING

Hunter-Trapper Reflector.—Our old friend the hunter-trapper fire again answers the purpose and gives added proof that it is the one essential cooking fire that a person needs to know. Build it as usual using slow-burning side-logs with a slow-burning fire of hardwood between to make a moderate bed of coals. As the coals begin to drop, put on the baking pan until the biscuits begin to rise. Then quickly hoist one log and place its ends on two butts or stones as thick as the log itself, as in A, Figure 57, turning the glowing surface down and a little forward. Set the baking pan upright close in front of the logs, leaning against a log or stone, and turn it as needed to bake evenly.

Hunter-Trapper Ovens.—Still another contribution of the hunter-trapper: Set up the hunter-trapper as usual except that the side-logs are placed at a wider angle, touching at the narrow end and wider apart than usual at the wide end, as in B, Figure 57. The fire is built in the narrow end. Place three or four lengths of logs over the fire and set up the biscuit pan perpendicularly between the logs as shown. Figure 57 tells the story clearly. When the bottom sides of the top log are well aglow, quickly rake the coals to the wide end, and set the pan on the hot ground beneath the top logs to finish the baking. You can cook the rest of the meal on the coals while the biscuits are baking.

And yet again: With a good bed of coals between the side-logs of a typical hunter-trapper fire, place the baking pan on top until the dough begins to rise, then lift both logs and place them on crosswise logs of equal size, hot side down as in C, Figure 57. Rake the coals aside and place the pan on the hot ground, and then roll logs or stones to cover the front and back openings. The two crosswise logs used to support the main logs may also be heated by placing them across the main logs before the fire is lighted; the burning surface should then be placed toward the pan as the oven is built.

Figure 58. REFLEC-TOR FIRE

Reflector Fire.—Figure 58 shows it. This is the traditional baking arrangement and is usually used with a reflecting baker. There is a bank of logs that throws the heat forward into the baker. Green uninflammable logs (see page 102) are required for the back wall, leaned against two poles driven in the ground, and a tall wigwam fire of quick-burning softwoods (page 98) is needed in front to furnish the quick blast of heat that baking demands. Two firedogs of green stuff extend out from the back wall on which to set the reflector baker. Have the baker in place before the fire is lighted.

OUTDOOR STOVES AND OVENS

Many and varied are the camp fireplaces and outdoor stoves if one has concrete with which to fashion them, of all levels of complexity and artistry, but these are for the parks, reservations, organized camps and picnic grounds, rather than the backwoods camp.* Even the simplest and most primitive of outdoor stoves is scarcely necessary in the bush, unless one is camping on the same spot for a long time. Boys and girls like them, however, particularly the making of them, so let us consider two elemental types which will provide delightful projects even though they may not be found important for the trail.

Trench Stove.—This is our old trench fire converted into a more permanent camp stove. Build it in the side of a hill, slabbing up the sides and back with flat rocks, and covering the top with sheet metal as in Figure 59. A section of an old kitchen-stove top makes a good top because it has holes and lids that can be removed in cooking. A chimney is essential for which a tile or a short section of an old kitchen-stove chimney may be employed. Make it small and save wood and work. To use it as an oven, build a hot fire in it, warm the biscuits on top until

Figure 59. TRENCH STOVE

they begin to rise, then rake out the coals, put in the pan, and close the opening with a rock slab.

Clay Ovens.—With the glamour of the adobe ovens of the Pueblo Indians in them, these clay ovens are ever popular among boys and girls in summer camps. What they may lack in practical value in backwoods camping they make up in strong romantic appeal. But they *will* bake biscuits—and bread.

A nailkeg or a small packing box forms the temporary core, over which wet clay is packed. Keep it small if you would have an oven that functions—the inside hole just large enough for the baking pan. To form the chimney hole, use a four- or five-inch softwood log around which cardboard has been wrapped and tied loosely. A hole for the door must be left as in Figure 60. Genuine clay is essential and should be piled on generously in making the walls and top. After

---

* For directions for making these in great variety see A. D. Taylor, *Camp Stoves and Fireplaces* (Washington: Government Printing Office, 1937). Also A. B. Good, *Park and Recreation Structures*, Volume II (Washington: Government Printing Office, 1938).

it has dried for a couple of days lift the chimney log out—it will slip out from the cardboard wrapping easily without disturbing the clay. Then build a gentle fire within to burn out the wooden core and complete the drying. Plug up the cracks with clay and the oven is ready.

To use: burn a hot fire within for a full hour, rake out the coals and sticks, put in the baking pan, and close the door.

Figure 60. CLAY OVEN

In case a nailkeg or packing box is not to be had, the core may be made of a pile of small straight sticks or poles. Drive four stakes to prevent them from rolling off, then lay the poles lengthwise of the oven, one above the other, until the shape of the desired opening is achieved. These are burned out by building a fire in front of the oven door when the clay is partly dry.

CAMPFIRES

Comes evening with dinner over and the need of fire for cheer, comfort, and light. Comes bedtime in the colder months with its need of fire for warmth. Two types of campfires are these, different from each other, and different from the cooking fires of pages past.

FIRES FOR CHEER AND LIGHT

Two or three loafing around in the evening will find light and friendship in the wigwam fire built in the Indian fashion, but the big crowd assembled in the council ring will need the council fire with its brilliance and dramatic flare.

The Indian Fire.—Here is where the lowly wigwam fire comes into its own. Build it of fine stuff as usual but when it comes to putting on the big poles, do not chop them but just pull the ends up onto the fire and let the poles radiate from it, as in Figure 61. When the ends are burnt, pull the poles up again. This is in the Indian tradition from the days when axes were not, but had they had axes I doubt if the

Indians would have cut the logs, for why chop when chopping is not needed? Dubbed by some as the *lazy man's fire*, it is not laziness to save work but just common sense. Softwoods are good for blaze but avoid the noisy and spitting evergreens.

The Council Fire.—Night and the glamour of council! the Redmen's symbolism, the beauty of costume, the compulsion of atmosphere, the intrigue of ritual, the eternal youth of primitive dancing—all under the great canopy of the night, with the sweet incense of fragrant earth-things and the thousand voices which only the Faithful hear and understand! And as the crowning glory, the sacred central fire!

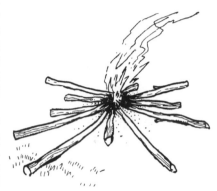

If ever a fire true in type and of expert making is needed, it is in the council ring. Failure of the fire comes nigh to meaning failure of council, and it is tragic to have the magic spell so broken.

Figure 61. THE INDIAN FIRE

What are the requisites?—a maximum of light and a minimum of heat! Story-tellers, dancers, players, and contestants cannot work up against a roaring blast furnace—bonfires will unmake the best of councils. Fires that soon go dead will leave a dramatic dance in darkness at its most appealing point and a week of rehearsal has gone for naught. It is doubtless true that more otherwise well-conceived councils have fallen from poor fire-building than from any other cause. The fire must be small in size and so designed as to light the farthermost corner of the scene.

It is the log-cabin or crisscross fire that meets these needs. There are three variations of it for use in the council ring, A in Figure 62 illustrating the first. It must be built of well-seasoned, brightly-burning wood, and frequently we can do no better than to use old lumber and packing-box stuff. Other woods must be finely split, for split sticks burn more brightly than do round ones. Hardwoods usually burn too slowly, and the softwoods must be watched to avoid the loudly crackling kinds; fortunately, however, the worst of the crackling is soon over and the fire settles down. On the bottom lay four round poles two inches thick and fifteen inches long and above them lay in crisscross fashion several layers of finely split sticks. All sticks should be exactly fifteen inches long and the fire built up to a height of fifteen inches, thus producing a square, box-like structure. Build a little pyramid of tinder on the ground under it and a little to one side of its center so that the fire-maker can throw his burning ball of tinder into it easily when the proper time in the ceremony

Figure 62. COUNCIL FIRES FOR LIGHT

arrives. Dampen the entire structure with kerosene so that with the first application of the lighted tinder the whole will go into blaze. Will true woodsmen use kerosene? The council fire calls for a combination of woodcraft and showmanship. Will a good showman refuse to use it if it makes the scene?

True, this crisscross of softwood will soon burn down, but the little fire lights up the ring amazingly and does not radiate too much heat for the opening ceremony. Before each dance or feature on the program a new supply of sticks is tossed on in roughly crisscross fashion. A large pile of prepared wood must be provided beforehand, well dampened with kerosene so that it flames immediately when put on. Good showmanship admonishes strongly against allowing the fire-tenders to replenish the fire during a dance or dramatic act—the attention attracted by them momentarily unmakes the atmosphere the

actors produce. The program can be so arranged as to provide intervals during which the fire is revived. Kerosene should never be poured
on a burning fire—dampen the sticks beforehand. This dampening is
an essential procedure for the sticks are put on when light is needed
and must immediately produce light.

After years of experimentation with every possible kind of log-
cabin arrangement, this crisscross of finely split softwood has been
the surviving method. But for a council ring that does not need so
vivid a light, such as one emphasizing contests and story-telling rather
than dancing, a more woodsy and slowly burning fire can be made
as in B, Figure 62. Make the log-cabin framework of seasoned poles
of hardwood that burns steadily (see page 99), the bottom layer
twenty-four inches long and the others progressively shorter, causing
the structure to taper. In between these logs the space is filled in with
split sticks as illustrated. When the split stuff burns out the framework continues to burn, and when more brightness is needed at a
particular moment a fresh supply of split sticks can be shoved between
the layers of the hardwood framework.

Still another variation of the council fire relies on a wigwam fire
for light and is seen in C, in Figure 62. The heavy framework is made
of very slow-burning green logs (see page 102) and merely serves to
hold in upright position the sticks of the central wigwam. When the
wigwam burns down it is replenished from the top.

NIGHT FIRES FOR WARMTH

A shelter with a wide open side is the warmest tent in cold weather
as we learned in Chapter I—the Baker Tent, or the Adirondack lean-to
among the permanent shelters—for the reason that they admit the
warm glow of the reflector fire. Just as the reflector fire bakes the
biscuits in the reflecting baker, so it warms the Baker Tent—indeed
the tent is built on the same plan as the oven. And the two fires are
identical except for size.

Cut four or five sections of an uninflammable green log six to eight
inches in diameter, each about four feet long. Drive two poles in the
ground at a slight slant and stack the logs against them as in Figure 63,
putting the heaviest on the bottom to prevent rolling off, and then
drive two more poles in front to hold all secure. When a large fire of
good hardwood logs is built in front, the upright wall will throw the
heat forward into the shelter. It will usually be necessary to rebuild

the fire once during the night and so a pile of reinforcements should be handy. For a long stay the backwall may be chinked with mud.

The fire should be close to the tent, the back wall not over seven feet from the opening.

Some campers recommend building the reflecting wall of dry hardwood on the theory that the logs will settle as they burn and thus

Figure 63. NIGHT FIRE FOR WARMTH

automatically feed the fire throughout the night. But there can be no assurance that it will so function and you will probably have to get up to tend it once anyway. So it is better to build a lasting wall out of one of the uninflammable woods on page 102, and build the fire of one of the good woods on page 99.

Sleeping Outside in Winter.—It depends on how cold it is. If you have no shelter in moderately cold weather the warm arrangement is to lie directly in front of the wall of the log reflector and *build the fire on the other side of you.* Between the fire and the reflector it is certain to be cozy. In colder weather, the fire may be built in front of the reflecting wall, and after it has been burning an hour, raked forward and the blankets spread on the warm earth between the wall and the fire. This is not practical if there is much ice on the ground because of the dampness. If we plan to sleep close to the fire in this way we must take particular pains to *avoid the spitfire woods.*

Heating a Tent.—Heat some stones in the fire, put them in a kettle, and turn the kettle upside down in the tent. Or if there is a groundcloth in the tent to prevent this, just set the kettle upright on a couple of poles. Were you ever in an Indian sweat lodge heated by rocks?

WOODCRAFT LIGHTS

Campfires fail us as sources of light when we are on the move—then we need torches. And they fail us inside when there is no fireplace—then we need lamps and candles.

Torches

There are two types, the natural torches that burn long and brightly by merely touching a match to them, and the artificial ones made by soaking some absorbent material with oil. It was the natural torch that lighted the moccasin trails of long ago—these are either of birch-bark or pitch.

Birch-Bark Torches.—The *waswagan* or torch most common among the woods-dwelling Indians consists merely of a coil of birch-bark eighteen inches long and two inches thick, as shown at A, in

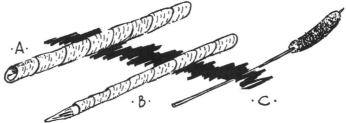

Figure 64. Torches

Figure 64. It will light the trail for fifteen minutes while walking. A strip of very heavy bark six inches wide and two feet long will make it, if merely twisted or coiled into a hollow tube as shown. Usually heavy birch-bark will coil naturally but string may be used to hold it if necessary. Light it and hold upright in the hand, and if it fades or begins to die out, turn it upside down and wave it for a second or two, then hold erect again. When it burns down near the hands a stick may be thrust in the bottom for a handle.

These were known as traveling torches among the Chippewas and were used by the men on the trail. Around camp the women used a "woman's torch" or "squaw torch" which was made the same but much thinner, about eighteen inches long and no bigger around than a broomstick, made by coiling thin birch-bark into a tube and tying. Into the bottom a stick was inserted, the end of which was pointed, as in B, Figure 64. When the squaw needed light at any particular point in her camp she would thrust the stick in the ground.

Pitched Torches.—While the birch-bark waswagan will burn for fifteen minutes, one made of pitch will produce an all-night light.

This is the *wawaceci-waswagan* of the Chippewas—*wawaceci* meaning deer, hence *deer-hunting torch.* Secure a stick the size of your
thumb and a foot long—the Chippewas preferred butternut or witch-
hazel—and pound all but the tip until the fibers loosen and separate.
Dip the stick in melted pitch, and while still soft wrap it with one
thickness of thin cloth; then smear pitch as thickly as possible over
the cloth. The unpounded or handle end is then pointed to stick in
the ground if desired. The Indians would set up this torch in the bow
of the canoe with a bark reflector behind it, for use in the night
hunting of deer.

For instructions for preparing the pitch see page 242.

Tallow Torches.—The tallow from a deer provided another kind of
torch used in deer hunting, although less brilliant than the pitched
stick. Put the tallow in a kettle, cover with boiling water and put on
the fire; skim off the water, cover again with boiling water, and skim
the second time. Pound the stick as for making the pitched torch,
dip in the tallow, cover with a thin cloth, and dip again—the process
is identical with that used for the pitched torch except that tallow
is used.

Pine-Knot Torches.—A pine knot is as good a torch as one would
want. These are the stumps of the branches and, being most imper-
ishable, good ones can be pulled out of old logs that are almost
completely decayed. If chopping is necessary cut deep and wide to
secure the whole pitched ball. Hold it by the stub of the branch
and light.

Cattail Torches.—Soaked in melted fat, a cattail provides the most
quickly made of torches—C in Figure 64. But if you can take the time
to produce a better one, dip it in melted pitch and wrap with thin
cloth as in making the pitched torches.

A Modern Torch.—It's modern in the sense that it needs a tin can
and kerosene, but it has a long and respectable history on the skating
ponds and coasting hills of the winter nights, as well as on the rafts
and boats of night fishermen and frog hunters. In the hands of a
skater as he glides through the night, this is a grand torch. Attach
the can to the end of a broomstick, or stick of similar size, by means
of a screw through its bottom. Pack old rags into the can until it is
about half full and then pour in all of the kerosene that the rag will
absorb; continue to pack rags until full, then turn inward the edge
of the can to grip the rags and soak again with coal-oil. A little coax-

ing will be necessary until the top layer of rags become burnt and charred, whereupon the rags will serve as a sort of wick and the torch will flame vividly for the better part of an hour.

LIGHTS FOR INDOORS

Grease Lamps.—One would need light badly to use these foul-smelling things, but what must be must be: Boil any kind of fat or animal grease a few minutes in water to free it from salt and then skim off the water. Pour the grease in a shallow dish or shell and hang a wick over the edge, made of a strand of cedar bark, a cotton string, or a rag. These sluts of the far frontier are always dingy, drippy and smoky.

To get rid of the dripping if not the odor, make a stiff wick from a slender branch of softwood four inches long by pounding it until the strands begin to loosen and then wrapping it with cotton cloth, or by wrapping a few strands of cedar bark in cloth. In the bottom of a cup or can put an inch of sand, pour the grease on top and insert the wick by sticking it in the sand. A little less messy than the simple slut but as smoky as ever!

Rush-Candles.—A rush or weed stalk with a large pithy center is needed in making these rush-candles that lighted many a cabin and camp in pioneer days. Remove the bark or outer stalk *except for a strip down one side*, exposing the pithy center. Drop in hot tallow and leaves until the pith soaks it up, then remove and dry. Set up in a candle holder of some sort and use as an ordinary candle.

Hand-Dipped Candles.—From the fat of mutton, beef, deer, elk, or any animal whose fat is tallow, the candles of the woods are made. And in the city, too, the dipping of candles is a joyous and profitable pastime for the family or club, especially as the Christmas season draws near. There is always a demand for these beautiful, artistically irregular, hand-made candles. Put the fat in a kettle, cover with water, and bring to a boil twice, skimming after each boiling. A few slices of raw potato boiled with the fat will help to clarify it, and if debris still remains the hot tallow may be strained through a cheesecloth. Candles made from pure tallow melt very easily, are drippy, and lose their shape in hot weather. And so it is better to mix the tallow with beeswax and a little alum if these items are to be had, using the following proportions: one pound of fat, one-half pound of beeswax, and one-quarter pound of alum. Heat these materials together by placing the kettle in a larger vessel of boiling water, and keep hot throughout the dipping.

Use ordinary candle wicking or make the wicks from cotton string. Double the string and twist it, then lay it over a broomstick and twist it again in the opposite direction, thus making a four-strand wick. In the woods a strand of shredded and boiled basswood bark may be used, prepared as described on page 258. A half-dozen wicks may be hung over the stick, spaced a couple inches apart, each hanging down a little farther than the length of the desired candle. Now lower the stick over the kettle so as to dip the wicks in the hot tallow, and then set the stick on supports near the fire so that the tallow will not dry too rapidly, placing papers underneath to catch any dripping. As soon as the tallow begins to harden, dip again and cool, repeating the process until the candles are of the desired thickness.

Hand-dipped candles are typically wider at the bottom than at the top because the hot tallow runs down and hardens there, and they are sure to be irregular in shape, all of which adds to their beauty. But if too lopsided, some of the wax may be scraped off with a knife, after which the candle should be given a final dipping.

Colored candles can be made simply by mixing a little dry paint powder obtainable at a hardware or paint store, into the hot tallow until it takes on the desired shade.

Trench Candles.—These are regarded as emergency tinder for the lighting of campfires in the rain but they do service also as an emergency light for the tent. They are made by dropping rolls of newspaper in melted paraffin as described earlier in this chapter—see page 108.

Bayberry Candles.—Not only light—pale, blue-green, and characteristic—but a delightful incense is sent forth from these most woodsy of candles, making of them an intriguing project for all who are interested in the crafts of the woods. It is from the berries of *bayberry* and its cousin, *wax myrtle*, that the "tallow" is obtained, gathered in the fall or any time during the winter. When the wax-coated berries are boiled in water the wax rises to the surface where it hardens as the water cools, to be skimmed and placed in another vessel. A second boiling may be necessary to rid it of all debris. It takes many berries to produce little wax, so gather generously while you are at it, but the bayberry wax can be made to go four times as far without losing too much of its aroma by mixing it with tallow or paraffin in the proportion of one part of bayberry wax to three of tallow. Candles are made from the hot wax just as other tallow candles: Obtain candle wicking or use cotton string for wicks as already described, doubling it and twisting loosely. Dip the wick in the hot tallow, let harden and dip again, and thus continue until a candle of the desired size is produced.

The dipping may be done from a broomstick as described for tallow candles, but since few bayberry candles will be made at one time, it may be handier to bend a wire into a hook by means of which the loop of the wick is caught and lowered into the tallow.

Figure 65.
A CANDLE
LANTERN

In pioneer days bayberries were ' rubbed on the bottom of hot flatirons in order to transmit the delicate perfume to handkerchiefs.

Candle Lanterns.—An unprotected candle is easy prey for the wind, but it would take a powerful blast to put out the lantern shown in Figure 65, and hence this rig is good for camp use. Saw off a round section from a branch of a tree for the base, or use a square block of wood. Drive four small-headed nails to support the lamp chimney and install two screw-eyes to which the wire handle is attached.

Other types of candle lanterns are described in Chapter XXIII.

PROTECTING YOUR MATCHES

More precious than ax, gun, tent or any other item in the duffel, yet one ducking in the lake or a heavy rain may ruin the whole supply of matches.

To go beyond the range of handy trading posts without absolute match protection spells a stupid and inexcusable disregard for the tragic consequence that an otherwise trivial water mishap may produce.

Two things to do: Carry a waterproof matchbox with an emergency supply of matches, and waterproof the main supply for regular use.

WATERPROOFING MATCHES

The large kitchen size is the match of the woods. Don't stint yourself on matches—figure your needs generously and then take more.

But no matter how many you take, an upset of the canoe can ruin them all, so they should be waterproofed.

The best way to waterproof a large supply of matches is with paraffin. Heat the paraffin, open the matchbox and pour the paraffin over the matches. Pinch the side of the box together with your fingers so that the paraffin does not bulge the box so much that the cover will not slip on, and if the liquid is so thin it leaks from the box, let it cool a little. The paraffin will harden into a cake and waterproof the whole box at once. When matches are needed a block can be broken off and the paraffin worked loose. Treated in this way the matches will survive a pretty good soaking.

There is another method of waterproofing matches, suitable for preparing a small supply. This consists of dipping the matches separately, or in bundles of a dozen held together with a string or rubber band, into one of the following solutions: ordinary shellac thinned with denatured alcohol, quick-drying cement such as used in crafts, or collodion from the first-aid kit. The pocket supply may be treated in this way but the main supply should be paraffined.

Waterproof Matchboxes

Be sure that it's waterproof—try it out by leaving it under water for a half day. Fill it with matches, carry it on your person constantly in a place where it cannot get away, *and never touch it except in case of dire need*. This holder is the last resort. Matches for regular use should be carried in the pocket.

In a pinch a waterproof matchbox can be made by filling a twelve-gauge shotgun shell with matches, and slipping a sixteen-gauge shell over it. But it is safer to buy an absolutely dependable one, preferably of the type with a screw cap.

Drying Wet Matches

The time-honored method of drying a damp match is to rub the head of it through your hair. If it is not soaked to the point where the head is pasty, the hair will quickly dry it.

FIRE WITHOUT MATCHES

Why?—in a world of matches? Ernest Thompson Seton answered well when a group of "practical" business-men questioned his zest for the rubbing-stick fire—said he, pointing to the ground, "You are thinking of the fire that is lighted down there," and pointing to his breast, continued, "I am thinking of the flame that is kindled in here!"

Impractical it is only to staid, prosaic oldsters who have forgotten that enchanted world of dreams called childhood!

Struggling for weeks and months—a year—before the days when commercial fire-by-friction sets came wrapped up in packages, experimenting and failing with countless woods and tinders, filling my room with a perpetual incense of woodsmoke that in itself was reward, I still recall that fervent youthful day when tiny coal turned to flame!— and happily the fire it kindled has never died! Must you say it is impractical?

But what of the fire that is lighted down there on the ground? As an emergency method of making fire in the woods, the conditions demanding it will seldom, perhaps never, occur, but many of us have demonstrated that, starting from scratch, an outfit can be made in the woods and fire produced within half an hour. Certain it is that if one's matches were ruined in the far wilds he would not need to go without fire, even though the task of locating the right wood and making the set were a long one—he would surely admit it was worth it, however long. The Indians who relied on the rubbing-stick fire carried the outfit with them, but so would you and I, if so caught, after once we had one made.

But while those fires will be few, if any, the learning of the way will kindle myriad fires—in the breasts of youth. And as a result countless hundreds of fires will be lighted *with matches* in the wilds throughout long lives of outdoor living, fires that, had the rubbing-stick way not been learned, might never have been kindled. And pictures in the rising smoke will be seen where otherwise there would be none.

The method of conjuring fire by friction is an oft-told tale, but once again in the hope that more fires within may be set ablaze:

The Rubbing-Stick Way

Woods.—These will make fire: *American elm, slippery elm, balsam fir, red cedar, white cedar, cypress, tamarack, basswood, cottonwood, poplar, sycamore, soft maple, white pine, willow.* And of the southern woods, particularly *yucca.*

Of the woods in the first sentence, American elm, balsam fir, and red cedar are the best. Of the remaining woods of that list, there is little to choose between them. But yucca is the best of all.

Among the Chippewa Indians to whom the rubbing of sticks was the common way of making fire, cedar was the choice. In fact, *gi-jik* (pronounced ge-zhek), the word for the fire-board, means cedar—in other words, they referred to the fire-board as "the cedar." Red cedar is better than white cedar. Cedar was also the preference of the Indians of the Northwest coast. The tribes of the eastern woods utilized elm and soft maple, the Hupa relied on willow, and in the southwest, the Apaches employed yucca while their Hopi neighbors used exposed cottonwood roots.

In locating wood in the forest it is a question not of the best of all woods, but of the best the particular spot offers. Any of the above woods will produce fire provided they are thoroughly dry and free from resin.

The Fire-Board.—A board of one of the above named woods three-eighths to one-half inch in thickness is needed. A foot in length and three inches in width makes a convenient size.

The Drill.—It measures about twelve inches in length and one-half to three-fourths inch in thickness. Saw off a square piece of that size from a board and whittle it to a roughly octagonal shape. Point the ends as shown in Figure 66.

The Bow.—A slightly curved branch of a tree makes the bow shown in Figure 66. It should measure at least twenty-seven inches in length for the best results. The *agimak* or fire-bow of the Chippewas was made of ash, although the kind of wood is unimportant. A heavy, strong thong of pliable leather or oiled rawhide makes the bowstring. The best way to attach it is to bore a hole in each end of the bow and run the thong through, tying it at one end and merely wrapping it around the other or handle end so that it can be easily tightened.

The Drill Socket.—This is important. A good one makes the process easy but a poor one may defeat us. A very hard substance must be inserted to permit the drill to spin with the least possible friction. In the city there is nothing to equal the glass top of a coffee percolator—it is made to order and only needs to be covered on the top with adhesive tape. The Indian often used a rock with a hole drilled in it. In a pinch a little block of very hard wood with a hole bored in it and well greased may be used, but it is better to fit a piece of metal such as a small thimble in the hole.

Tinder.—The best is *red cedar bark*, sanctioned by Woodland Indian tradition and verified by modern experimentation. *White cedar bark* is a very close second. Pound the bark, roll it with the sole of the shoe, and otherwise work it until it is a fine shredded mass, then rub it between the hands to permit the dust to fall out, leaving the fuzzy shreds. Other excellent tinders are the inner barks of *chestnut* and *slippery elm*, and *cottonwood bark; field mouse nests;* and *red* or *white cedar wood* finely scraped with a piece of broken glass.

Shredded rope or *twine* makes good tinder but works better if a little shredded bark is placed in the center.

To Make Fire.—Sharpen the drill to a point and wrap the bowstring around it as in Figure 66. Place the point three-eighths of an inch from the edge of the fire-board and drill a small hole. Then cut a notch with a knife bringing the point of it to the exact center of the hole. A slightly U-shaped notch is better than a V. The notch may be cut first but it is easier to bring the point to the center of the fire hole if the hole is started

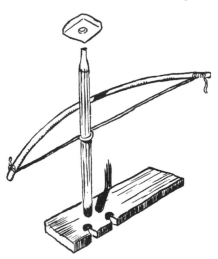

Figure 66. FIRE-BY-FRICTION SET

first. The bottom of the drill should be pointed only when starting the hole and thereafter should remain in the bluntly rounded shape that the friction creates.

Lay the tinder on a chip of dry wood and place the notch of the fire-board directly over its center. Set up the fire outfit as shown in Figure 66—note that the drill is on the *outside* of the thong away from the bow. Kneel on the right knee, place the left foot firmly on the fire-board to hold it immovable, grasp the drill-socket in the left hand, and *keep the left wrist firmly against the left leg to prevent wobbling.* Make long even strokes with the bow held in the right hand.

A spin or two and smoke begins to rise from the pit. Press harder with the left hand on the drill-socket and continue until black smoking powder appears in notch. Then lift the drill out carefully—to throw it or drop it may scatter the powder. Pick up both tinder and drill-board, blow gently into the notch, then lift off the board to find a large glowing coal on the tinder. Blow this up into a flame. With perfect tinder a puff or two is all that is needed. If coaxing is necessary, wrap the tinder gently around the spark and blow into it a time or two, then turn it around and give it a puff on the opposite side. Swinging the tinder in a circle over the head is dramatic but seldom necessary.

Remember these points and you can't fail, provided the wood is right:

1. Don't let the fire-board move—press hard with the left foot.
2. Keep the drill steady by pressing the wrist against the leg.
3. Take long strokes with the bow, using its full length.
4. Press harder on the drill with each stroke.
5. Lift off the drill carefully so as not to scatter the black powder forming the coal.

And one point more: The Chippewas have it that if the One Above is to send fire, *the top of the drill must be rubbed once each side of the nose* before it is placed in the drill-socket! This is more than superstition, for there is just enough oil there to cause the drill to whirl smoothly in the socket.

By Flint and Steel

No steel but just two pieces of hard rock (flint and iron pyrites) were used by the timber Indians in ancient days to produce sparks. But the steel of later years simplified the task.

These are needed:

1. A piece of flint, quartz, or other very hard rock, just large enough to grasp conveniently in the fingers.
2. A piece of hardened steel, such as a broken file or the back of your jackknife blade.
3. A little charred cotton cloth, charred cotton rope, or lamp-wick (the Indians used "punk" or dry rotted wood).
4. Tinder as for the rubbing-stick fire.

To char the cotton cloth or twine, set fire to it and when well ablaze stamp the foot gently on it to extinguish it. Then select small bits of the blackened cloth.

Place the charred cotton in the center of your cedar-bark tinder. Hold your jackknife or other steel in the left hand vertically over it and about an inch above it. Strike the edge of the flint or other rock against the steel with a downward motion sending the spark onto the charred cotton. When the cotton begins to smolder and glow, fan it and blow it gently until the tinder bursts into flame. With practice you can hold the tinder in the palm of your left hand and the steel above it in the fingers of the same hand.

UNWELCOME FIRE

A don't or two, for when the Thunderbird crashes his mighty wings together and the terrifying flash of his darting eyes dazzles the earth, there is menace to the camper, more by far than to the city dweller—menace that is often belittled by those who have never seen a great tree shattered by a smashing bolt.

If you would be safe with the Thunderbird in angry mood you will watch the following danger points:

1. *Stay away from wire fences*—lightning will travel several yards along a wire fence to endanger the lives of any living creature coming in contact with it.

2. *Do not take refuge under a lone tree* in an open field.

3. In selecting a camping spot in the woods, *avoid extra tall trees.* Sooner or later every tree raising its head above its neighbors will be struck.

4. In open fields stay off your feet—the lightning will not seek you out if you make yourself inconspicuous.

CHAPTER VII

CAMPFIRE GADGETS

NOW TO THE TASK of housekeeping around the fire. Simple housekeeping—for camping is of the earth and relies on earthy things.

Artificial gadgets there are, and many—a swing around an outfitting store, or a glance at its catalogue, will reveal a host of devices designed to add comfort to camping, in which their inventors have invested much camping wisdom and a greater amount of camping nonsense. All of these would doubtless be helpful and convenient sometime, some place. But to attempt to haul along every promising knickknack would be to make a pack-horse out of oneself—and all unnecessarily. For aside from axes, knives, food bags, and a first-class aluminum cooking outfit which nestles and fits into a carrying bag, with a homemade inspirator and a pair of canvas gloves inside, there is only one gadget associated with cooking that could be regarded in the class of the essential or worth its place in the duffel—the wire grate or grid.

There are, however, many gadgets of the earth—sticks and stones and the like—that are priceless but still cost nothing, and do not have to be hauled. Let us look over these:

KETTLE SUPPORTS

Somehow the kettle must be hung or supported over the fire and insured against an upset. There are many ways:

WIRE GRATE

It's not indispensable by any means but is a great convenience and of such practical import as to justify its weight and bulk. With it we can dispense with the side-logs of the hunter-trapper fire for ordinary cooking, and with all other complicated fires, and need only the simple wigwam and crisscross fires. Build the crisscross fire as usual and set the grid over it—put the kettle on the grid and light up the fire. When it burns down to coals, force the wire legs of the grid down into the ground to lower it for cooking the meat. When more wood is needed it should be shoved under in two layers, crisscross, to permit ample air for quick burning. In a camp for several days, the hunter-trapper fire may be desirable, and on it the grill can be laid crosswise of the two side-logs to hold the small pans.

The wire grid is an excellent grill for cooking steaks without a skillet. Put the steak on it over a good bed of hickory coals and you will have a steak without an equal—hickory somehow seems to give

Figure 67. WIRE GRATE

steaks a characteristic flavor. Of course any of the hardwoods will do.

There are two types of wire grills, one merely with wire legs and open sides, the other with metal sheets down the sides. The latter is the better in that it conserves and reflects the heat, but it is at the same time the heavier. The ordinary one with open sides will answer every purpose for a shifting camp when the outfit must be hauled.

Secure a canvas case for it so that the soot and black from it will not foul the outfit in the packs.

SINGLE-STICK POT-HANGERS

The simplest and most quickly tossed together device for hanging a kettle is shown in its various forms in Figure 68, called the *wambeck, spygelia* or *waugan-stick,* depending on which part of the northern or eastern woods you are in and the type of native with whom you are talking. The Indians have a word for it in that territory, too—*chiplok-wagan* or *kit-chiplok-wagan,* of which waugan-stick is obviously a corruption. This device handles one kettle only and is good for a little lunch fire.

But mark this well: The waugan must be torn down ere you leave the spot, else the Night-spirits will trail you with ill luck the rest of your days—at least, so an old Indian once told me who had known a man who once forgot!

The trouble with the log or stone supports in A and B is their lack of dependability—many a teapot has been spilled when the supporting stick slipped from over or under an uncertain stone. That is why C

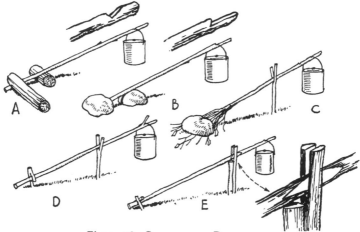

Figure 68. SINGLE-STICK POT-HANGERS

is a safer way—the twigs are left on the tip of the shoot to grip the stone, and the pot hung from the butt end.

When the forked sticks in D are not at hand, a straight upright may be split, and a second pole driven to prevent the waugan from slipping down too far, as shown in E.

Indian Waugan.—But the Indians can beat any of these: Always doing it the easy way they set up the rig shown in Figure 69, using

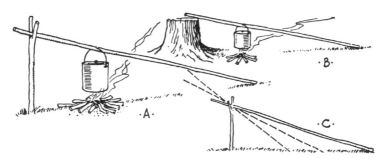

Figure 69. INDIAN WAUGAN

either a forked stick or an old stump. The height of the kettle is regulated by changing the angle of the pole, as indicated by the dotted lines in C, and a nick in the pole with a knife catches the pot handle. All of the waugans we have described are really in the Indian manner, and there seems to be no good reason for singling out this one with the label of an Indian waugan, other than the fact that it is particularly characteristic of the red woodsmen and seldom seen in use outside the Indian country.

A Stone Pot-Holder.—In this business of camping we use what is handy and never go a-foraging for any particular kind of an object that does not turn up after a quick look around. If a stone is handy

Figure 70. STONE POT-HOLDERS

there is no need of a waugan-stick. Just set the teapot on the stone and build a wigwam fire around it as in Figure 70. Or if there is a skillet besides the pot, place three stones in a tight cluster and build the fire around them and in the crevices. Figure out some way to do it with what you have and don't waste time hunting for what isn't to be had.

Adjustable Crane.—Stuart Thompson is the inventor of this handy gadget for lowering and raising a pot at will. Accommodating one kettle only it is good for a stew which must be cooked a long time with much rebuilding and burning down of the fire. Set up a crotched stick with pegs driven around its base to make rigid as in Figure 71.

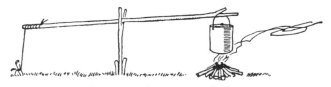

Figure 71. ADJUSTABLE CRANE

Then place the crane midway of its length in the crotch. The fire is built under the thin end and the butt end is attached to a stake driven in the ground directly under it by means of a rope. By wrapping the rope around the butt of the crane the rope is shortened or lengthened and the kettle hoisted or lowered accordingly. A handy rig!

About Crotched Sticks

The picture-book crotched stick with the two prongs spreading into a perfect Y as in A, Figure 72, is a rare item in the woods and if the hanging of the kettle depended on finding one I fear many a tea pail would never get boiled. And when one is uncovered it is apt to be of scant worth because it is next to impossible to drive it into solid ground without splitting it, there being no direct line of wood to

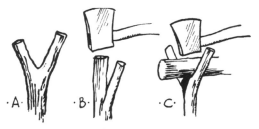

Figure 72.

carry the force to the ground. Better to get a straight pole with a branch going off to one side obliquely, as shown in B, which can be pounded with abandon with no fear of splitting. In case a Y-shaped crotch must be driven, the only safe way to accomplish it is to lay a pole through the crotch and pound on the pole, as illustrated at C in the drawing.

In pointing a stick to drive in the ground, the custom in the woods is to cut it on four sides thus making a square-sided point rather than a round one. A guide once told me in my boyhood days that such a point drives easier than a round one. I can't vouch for that, but I follow the custom—such a peg is quicker and easier to make anyway.

The Standard Crane

The typical camp kitchen with its crane for the kettles in Figure 73 is seen nine times out of ten in backwoods camps. It is substantial and handy but a second choice in my experience to the Chippewa kitchen racks in Figure 75, especially if one is setting up to stay at the spot for several days.

In cutting the forked poles for the uprights, select those with several branches protruding and do not trim them off flush, but allow them to extend a few inches to serve as convenient hooks for kettles, cups, towels, etc. An assortment of pot-hooks should be hung on the lengthwise lug-pole, made as described in a later paragraph. Even if

Figure 73. THE STANDARD CRANE

a hunter-trapper fire is used with its side-logs for the kettles, the crane will be a handy addition.

In case forked sticks cannot be located the crane may be erected by splitting the top of the uprights enough to accommodate the end of the lug-pole when it has been flattened down as in B. Or the end of the lug-pole may be split and slipped over the thinned-down top of the upright as in A. These methods should seldom be necessary except in parks and reservations, however, for the oblique forks are everywhere in the woods, and are not only handier to erect but offer the possibility of several convenient hooks for hanging the kettles as shown.

Movable Cranes.—A clever device permitting the swinging aside of the lug-pole so that it will be out of the way when not in use is shown in Figure 74. The kettles can be swung aside without handling them when fuel is being added or when the meal is cooked and ready to dish up. This serves every purpose that the standard crane accomplishes and is no more trouble to erect.

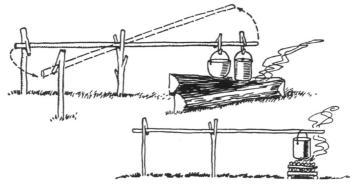

Figure 74. Movable Crane

Chippewa Outdoor Kitchens

From my old Chippewa friends, born woodsmen all, I learned the making of these simple outdoor kitchens without an equal, saw them in use outside countless scores of waginogans over a wide frontier, preferred to all others by families whose every meal means cooking on a campfire. A little fussy, may be the first reaction on glancing at the types in Figure 75, but they are handier by far than the stereo-

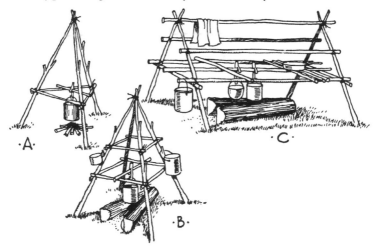

Figure 75. Chippewa Kitchens

typed crane and take but little longer to build—for a camp of several days they can't be beat.

No novelty is the tripod in A, for tripods have hung kettles no end in the camping of children, but it is the least prevalent among the timber Indians. It has its points—strong, secure, upset-proof. The kettles may be hung from the apex in story-book fashion, but preferably from a pole laid across the horizontal braces.

Better is the four-pole frame in B. Its advantages are manifold: There are many prongs and stick ends on which to hang kettles, cups, and skillets; many poles on which to spread dishcloths, towels, and wet clothing; a movable lug-pole for the kettles which can be shoved about at will. The cross-sticks are tied to the corner poles with thongs of basswood bark or with twine. These pointed kitchens outside the picturesque dome-shaped waginogans of bark are the mark of old-time Indian woodcraft.

Best is the larger frame with the long poles shown in C. It is more commodious, with more room for hanging. A few sticks laid across the lower horizontal poles at one end will make a platform for utensils. The top pole is five feet high and the lower lengthwise poles about three feet high, thus offering no interference to movement when setting, or bending over, the fire. Food hung on the poles at night is safe from prowling animals if a smoldering fire is left, for no wild animal relishes the odor of smoke. Such a kitchen is well worth the half hour to tie it up if we are to camp on the spot for a few days.

The Indian purpose of the many horizontal poles in these kitchens is to hang strips of meat and fish for smoking and drying, which use will not interest the camper but he will find they will not come amiss day in and day out, and will be put to a score of unanticipated uses.

POTHOOKS

By this we mean *pot-claws, gibs, crooks, trammels, hakes, hangers,* or *chips,* as you choose. Figure 76 shows them. Some are simple and practical, others designed to combine handicraft with usefulness.

A, B and C are the common types of the white woodsmen, B and C permitting raising or lowering the kettle by means of the notches or hooks at different levels.

The Indians are more inclined to D and E. That in D is made by bending a not-too-heavy green branch and heating it in the fire to set the curve, then lashing the end to the stick with basswood-bark thongs. For these pothooks the Chippewas prefer *chokecherry*. The loop in E is made by the bark of the stick, tied as illustrated. The

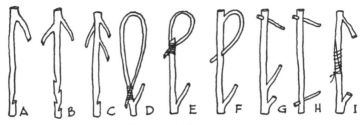

Figure 76. POTHOOKS

bend in F is also set by heating and the end is pegged through the stick.

The hooks in G, H and I are more interesting as handicraft projects than as work-a-day pot-hangers in the woods.

In making a pothook such as A, the notch for the kettle bail should be cut on the same side of the stick as the prong used for the hook.

Figure 77. HUNTER-TRAPPER SUBSTITUTE

HUNTER-TRAPPER SUBSTITUTE

If side logs are not to be had for the hunter-trapper lay, two green poles may be laid in crotched sticks as in Figure 77, on which to support the pans. The crotches should be about six inches up from the ground. Is this as efficient as the side-logs? No --the logs hold the heat.

RUSTIC COOKING UTENSILS

Broilers and grills for the steaks, spits for the barbecue, planks for the fish, toasters for the bread—no need for kitchen utensils when one has a knife or an ax in the woods:

WOODCRAFT BROILERS

An ever popular craft in camps is the making of these hand grills from green branches, and no hotel grill can broil a better steak.

Look at the assortment in Figure 78, all approximately the size of a tennis racket:

Type A is an excellent substantial broiler, made from a double-forked stick. Twist the ends of the outer forks together as shown, and hold in place with cross-sticks of the size of your little finger or a trifle smaller. If the outer forks are so stiff that they tend to spring apart when twisted together, stick them in the fire to set the curve, but do this before the cross-sticks are installed.

Type B is also made of a double-forked stick, but in using it keep

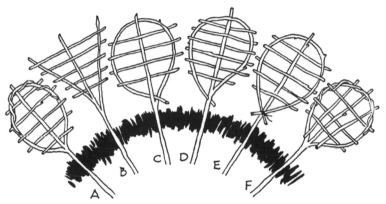

Figure 78. WOODCRAFT BROILERS

your eye on your steak, for this one lacks the sturdiness of those with curved ends.

Type C is made from an ordinary forked stick, much easier to find than the double forks. Double the outside branch around and stick its end in the crotch—the spring will hold it very firm. If the crotch is not at the right angle to catch the end, peg the end as in Type D or lash it.

Type D is made of a similar fork but with the end pegged through a hole in the main stick.

Type E is sometimes the only choice because forked sticks are not always in sight. It is made of two sticks: Bend the loop over the straight stick as shown, and place the cross-sticks under and over the straight stick alternately as illustrated, relying on the pressure to hold all secure.

Type F is an excellent grill, made just like A, of a double-forked stick, except that two additional lengthwise sticks are added.

Important to remember: (1) *Avoid nut-bearing trees* (except hickory)—they are bitter. (2) *Avoid rhododendron, laurel, poison oak, poison sumac*—the last two are poisonous and there are grave suspicions that the first two are likewise. (3) *Avoid ash*—it burns better green than dry and will catch fire. Use green sticks of sweet woods, preferably hardwoods.

GRILLS

Woodcraft Grills.—A few straight green sticks of the size of your little finger laid across the side-logs of the hunter-trapper fire, with a good bed of coals between, will make a first-class woodcraft grill for steaks and chops. Or laid across a trench fire, or across a fire-in-a-hole of the size of a washbasin, as in Figure 79! *Watch the wood selected*

Figure 79. WOODCRAFT GRILLS

for the twigs—those to be avoided are listed under "Woodcraft Broilers" in the preceding paragraph.

Figure 80. GRAVEL-SCREEN GRILL

Gravel-Screen Grill.—For a long stay, or for the cooking-out kitchen in an organized camp, six feet of heavy gravel screening will find many uses. Stretched across a standard trench fire and supported by poles laid along its edges as in Figure 80, it makes an excellent grill for steaks, chops, and wieners. Over a pit of deep hot coals and made rigid by occasional iron crossbars beneath, it does duty as a barbecue for roasts, chickens, etc.

A basket made of it is ideal for holding the food in the imu pit, or merely a square of it laid in the pit will support the food and provide an easy method of lifting it out. A garden rake is the proper tool with which to lift or move gravel screen when hot.

Woodcraft Spits

Spits for Broiling.—These are hiking gadgets, interesting only for a single meal in the open. Children like to spear a piece of steak or a chop on a stick and hold it over the fire. They should be taught better methods but if it must be done, the spit should be a forked stick with the two prongs whittled down and pointed as in A, Figure 81, and should be run through the narrow way of the meat as shown.

Figure 81. Spits

Better to kabob the meat: Cut it up in chunks *one inch* in width and string it on a sharpened twig as in C, leaving a little space between for well done and no space for rare. These may be cooked as kabobs: all solid meats (with bacon and onions between), oysters, cheese, and bananas. Each is better with a strip of bacon strung along. Hold the stick over the coals, suspend it on forks as in D, or lay it on the ground over a fire hole as in E.

The omnipresent hike wieners should be impaled on a forked stick as in B, and an oyster kabob is also set up on such a stick.

Barbecue Spits and Slings.—A green pole of sweet hardwood an inch or a little less in thickness makes the spit, preferably one with an off-shooting branch to serve as a convenient crank as indicated in A, Figure 82. If in doubt as to its "sweetness," taste it! Peel the bark and point one end. If it's to be a chicken to be barbecued, run the spit through it and out the neck, then tie the legs firmly to the spit. If cooking on the level of the ground drive two crotches as in Figure 82, of such height that the chicken will be about six inches from the hot coals. Turn it rather constantly but slowly by means of the crank and in an hour it should be ready to take up. A fire in a hole is better for barbecuing—drive the crotch pegs either side of the pit, or lay poles either side of it on which to rest the spit. A whole row of chickens may be impaled on the same spit if the crowd is large and hungry, the spit to be placed lengthwise over a fire built in a trench.

Remember that in barbecuing the meat must be well basted every

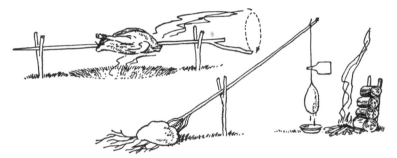

Figure 82. BARBECUE SPITS AND SLINGS

few minutes and requires regular watching and turning. For large barbecues a new dust mop is the ideal basting tool, and for small ones, a paint brush or a cotton dish-washing mop.

If it's a beef roast or other solid meat, don't try to impale it by running the pointed stick through, but slit it open, lay in the spit, and tie firmly together with cord.

The gravel screening recommended so often in this chapter makes an excellent barbecue rack. Lay it over a trench fire filled with good coals, secure it by logs either side, and lay on the meat.

Seton's spinning sling is one of the cleverest of barbecuing devices, saving much work because it does its own turning. Suspend the meat from a cord attached to a rig of some sort, as in B, Figure 82, and just above the meat attach a foot-square paddle of wood or bark. The breeze turns the paddle and keeps the meat spinning until the cord is wound up and then it reverses direction and unwinds of its own accord, repeating the process endlessly. The meat should be a little to one side of the fire, with a pan underneath to catch the drippings, and a backlog reflector should be erected to increase the heat.

TOASTERS

To get the bread toasted with the least possible effort, and well toasted too, use the method shown in A, Figure 83—merely thrust

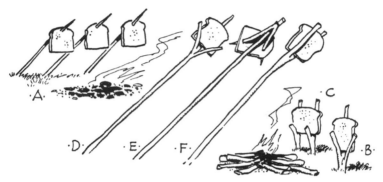

Figure 83. TOASTERS

a slender sharpened twig through each piece of bread and stick it in the ground before the fire, making a row around the edge of the ashes, and when one side is toasted slip the bread off and reverse it. If you like to whittle and combine handicraft with cooking use one of the other methods. The gadgets in A, B and C are stuck in the ground and do their own holding, while those in D, E and F are held in the hand.

WOODCRAFT PLANKS

It's really not a plank but a slab split off a sweet hardwood, about three inches thick and a little longer and wider than the steak or fish. To cook a chop merely set the "plank" over the fire until the sap begins to simmer, then put on the chop and proceed as if it were a grill.

To plank a fish (or a steak) four or five holes must be bored in the slab and sharpened wood pegs made to fit in them. Set the plank up against a reflecting fire until it is piping hot. While it is heating, split the fish down the *back* and spread it out, leaving the belly

Figure 84. PLANK FOR FISH

intact. Then working fast, remove the sizzling slab, cover it generously with grease, lay on the dry fish flesh side up, add a few strips of bacon for basting, and then peg it down by running the pegs through into the holes as in Figure 84. Set it up in front of the reflecting fire until it becomes flaky, when it is ready to season and eat from the slab.

SKEWERS FOR BARBECUING FISH

The day when your luck is good and you catch a big one is the time to try a fish barbecue, for small ones are better cooked in other ways. Build a long, narrow fire and pile on plenty of hardwood, starting it long before it's time to begin cooking in order to produce a deep bed of coals. Then erect above it the horizontal pole resting on props of some sort as in Figure 85.

Figure 85. BARBECUING FISH

Scale and clean the fish as usual but remove the backbone by slitting either side of it *from the inside of the fish* and being careful not to cut through the outer skin. Flatten out the fish and season it. Then whittle two skewers of sweet hardwood, a half inch or less in thickness depending on the size of the fish, and at least two feet long—they should extend at least eight inches either side of the fish. Insert these through the fish as in Figure 85, and lean the skewers against the horizontal pole with the flesh side of the fish toward the fire as shown. When the meat becomes flaky, turn it over and heat the back side for a little while. Remember that barbecuing requires basting, and this can be done automatically by pegging a few strips of bacon to the fish.

Many fish may be barbecued in this way at the same time by lining them up on both sides of a large fire.

GADGETS FOR HANDLING HOT OBJECTS

Essential to every cooking fire is a *"stove-poker," fire-tongs*, and *cooking gloves*. These should all be kept together on the crane, always in the same place. And if hot rocks are to be handled, as would be the case with a fire in a pit, *rock-tongs* will be needed also.

Any green pole of broomstick size will do for the poker, but be sure to have one for that purpose only and keep it in the same place always.

Fire-Tongs

These are made from a three-foot green pole of broomstick size bent almost double, as A, Figure 86. Heat helps to bend it: Bend

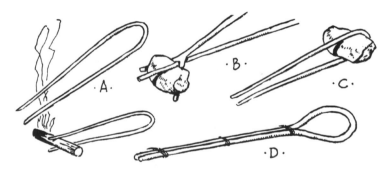

Figure 86. Gadgets for Handling Hot Rocks

it as far as possible without breaking, then hold the bent section in the fire until hot; then bend farther and farther until the ends are almost together and continue to heat until the bend is set and the tongs keep their shape. Hang the tongs on the crane where they will always be within reach and handy for picking up burning sticks and butts.

COOKING GLOVES

Convenience in campfire cooking demands a pair of ordinary canvas gloves, or better still a pair of Indian-made buckskin gloves. Put them on when you start the meal and leave them on throughout the cooking, thus permitting yourself to handle the kettles and burning sticks with abandon, without the necessity of reaching each time for a rag with which to protect the fingers.

These gloves should be used for cooking only and should be kept clean, never in contact with fish or other smelly or messy material. When on the go, they are carried in the cooking kit.

TONGS FOR HOT STONES

A forked stick is the traditional shovel for shoving hot rocks in and out of the fire-pit. If the rocks must be actually lifted, an additional stick inserted through the crotch of the forked stick from below, as in B, Figure 86, will do the trick. A small hot rock may be manipulated with the curved end of the fire-tongs as in C, Figure 86—this was the method used by many of those Indian tribes that cooked food in watertight baskets by submerging hot stones in the water, but the bent stick used by them was usually longer and bent to a more abrupt angle than in the typical fire-tongs.

Still another Indian gadget for lifting hot rocks in and out of a kettle consists of a bent stick with a circular bend in the end as D in Figure 86. In making this a slender, limber stick is soaked for a few days, then bent around a pole and tied as shown, later to be slipped off the pole as the curve becomes set.

RUSTIC COOKING ALTARS

On the trail one has no choice but to bend and kneel over his fire on the ground, taking the knee cramps and backaches with a grin. But in the pioneer unit of an organized camp where groups will cook every day for long periods, the wise camper out of regard for his back will bring his fire up to a handy level by means of a fire altar. Not only fewer aches and cramps in this arrangement, but there is safety in it too, for the fire is elevated, confined, and out of contact with combustible ground debris.

An assortment of styles is displayed in Figure 87. Build the walls of logs in log-cabin fashion with corners slightly notched and spiked with eight-inch spikes, and then fill the center with earth and rocks—careful notching is unnecessary in that the cracks between the logs will do no serious damage. If the back wall is extended up two-and-one-half feet above the top, as in A, it will serve as a reflector for baking. An altar eighteen inches high is a good elevation for little folks, as shown in B, but adults will prefer one two-and-one-half feet in height as in A. Make it generous in size—four-and-one-half to five feet square. The top should be well packed with hard earth and

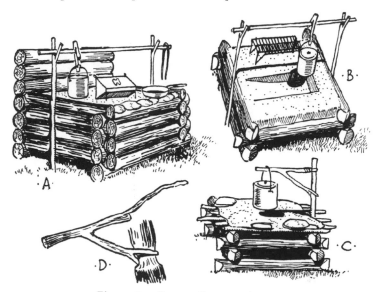

Figure 87. RUSTIC COOKING ALTARS

kept immaculately swept—a daily sprinkling with water will soon produce a floor-like smoothness and hardness.

Erect a solid crane on substantial forked poles, permanently set in the ground at the sides. A trench may be made in the top and lined with stones as in B if you are given to the use of the trench fire. Otherwise a movable wire grate or grid may be set on top. Sometimes these altars are made with a permanent bean hole in them, with a flat slab or rock covering it, used as a fireless cooker.

The altar in C is equipped with a swinging crane, a very appealing craft project for boys and girls but of scant practical value on a permanent altar because it handles but one or two kettles. The shape of the forked stick from which it is made is shown in D. The lower fork rests in a groove cut around the upright pole, and the upper stick is attached to the upright by means of a loop of bark which was peeled loose from the extension of the stick before it was sawed off. The bark is wrapped around the upright and tied to the horizontal pole. The crane may thus be swung aside when not in use. The trees whose bark may best be trusted for strength and pliability are basswood and slippery elm.

No logs to be had, the altar may be built of rocks but this usually calls for concrete unless flat rocks are present in abundance.*

---

* For descriptions of many types of permanent and ornamental outdoor fireplaces useful in parks and organized camps, see A. D. Taylor, *Camp Stoves and Fireplaces* (Washington: Government Printing Office, 1937). Also A. B. Good, *Park and Recreation Structures*, Vol. II (Washington: Government Printing Office, 1938). Also G. A. Sanderson and Virginia Rich, *Barbecue Book* (San Francisco: *Sunset Magazine*, 1938).

CHAPTER VIII

AXMANSHIP

THE AX represents the second period of American woodcraft. With no keen edge to hew his timber, the red woodsman lived well and happily in the truly woodcraft way. But a new day dawned to reveal a different world when came the ax. Speeding up the tempo of life, creating a more substantial world, the ax relegated to the seven thousand years of yesterday the bark and hide of the Indian's shelter so far as permanent dwellings were concerned, and supplanted the roving uncertainty of life with the clearing of fields for grain.

Ax and rifle—these subdued the American wilderness in the hands of the early woodsmen. To argue which was the more essential is patter as idle as tweedle-dee and tweedle-dum. And both are important in the far bush today. But you take the rifle and give me the ax!

I like axes. I like to have one near me always to speak of simple living in a city-world of mad and whirling things.

SELECTING AND CARING FOR THE AX

The golfer has his favorite clubs, the baseball player his peculiar style and weight of bat, the canoeist his particular shape and length of paddle—and so, too, the woodsman has a fondness for a certain style and weight of ax and often refuses to work with any other. It is no uncommon sight to see an old-timer of the woods go through the whole supply of axes in a store and cast them all aside in disgust. Particularly sensitive is he to the hang of the handle or helve, but while casual choppers will not be troubled with this type of temperament, one thing must be watched—the line of the blade as you sight along it must be in direct line with the center of the handle—see Figure 91.

Confusing indeed is the maze of shapes and styles of axes, each with myriad variations. In pioneer days axes were made locally by blacksmiths, each according to his own ideas, and consequently a tradition has developed in each locality favoring the style started and used in the early years by the smiths in that vicinity. Thus we have the Maine, New England, Kentucky, Michigan, Wisconsin, Western, California, Puget Sound, and many other styles manufactured by present-day makers of axes. A glance at a catalogue of axes will give an indication of the variety of standard styles. Manufacturers of axes, however, relieve the average camper from confusion in selecting from this maze by featuring one style of ax in each size for general sale, unless otherwise instructed, and this style is usually of the Michigan pattern or a slight variation of it, which shape is probably best suited for average use.

AXES FOR THE CAMPER

Essential to everyone going into the woods is a good camp-ax or hatchet—and a large ax is usually needed also. Single-bit or double-bit? Size and shape? Let us see:

Camp Hatchet.—It depends on the camper—his age, experience, and kind of camping he expects to do. And tastes vary. But a first-class hand-ax is a No. 1 item in any camper's duffel. It deserves attention—and discrimination in selection.

The beginning days of boys and girls will find adequate the typical camp or scout ax displayed in A, Figure 88, of which there are many makes. Sturdy and rugged, it will stand the type of abuse that inexperience is sure to give it during learning days. But not for long will this ax satisfy—the adult camper, and the experienced boy and girl, will want a better tool, a hand-ax of more suitable design for chopping.

My vote goes to the type of camp-ax shown in B. Note the long, slender handle—*eighteen inches over all.* Light, fast, perfectly balanced, the ease and speed with which chopping can be done with it is remarkable. But what of its weight? Its head is no heavier than the typical camp-ax of the type in A, its slender handle but slightly heavier. Its one disadvantage is the length of the handle when carried on the belt, but that is insignificant as compared to the saving of labor in chopping. It is at once a one-handed and a two-handed ax, as light as the average one-handed hatchet, yet with a handle long enough for two-handed swinging in felling small timber. No larger ax is really needed to supplement it on a camping trip in the bush.

This is not an ax for a young boy or girl. A highly tempered head will not stand abuse without chipping and a keen edge may lead to injury. Nor should it be given unwarranted abuse by anyone. I often

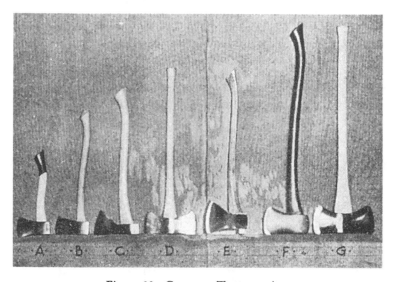

Figure 88. COMMON TYPES OF AXES

A—Small Camp-ax (Collins); B—Camp-ax with eighteen-inch handle (Marble); C—Hudson's Bay Ax (Collins); D—Cruiser Double-bit (Marble); E—Cedar Ax (Plumb); F—Full-sized Pole Ax (Plumb); G—Full Double-bit (Knot Klipper).

carry an additional hand-ax of the type of A if on a trip when weight does not matter, for there are many uses for a knock-about ax in camp for which a good ax should not be used. This permits the saving of the ax in B for chopping.

These axes may be obtained with a shorter handle of sixteen inches, or a longer handle of twenty inches. But you can't beat the eighteen-inch handle for balance.

There are many fine campers who follow the Nessmuk tradition in preferring a tiny ax of "vest-pocket" size.* Miniature models of the ax in B, identical except for size, are available for those who want a diminutive size of extreme lightness. But I'll stay with the eighteen-inch one and save work in the end—it does everything.

The Double-Bit Ax.—It's dangerous! But like many dangerous things it is a joy and a pleasure. Its advantages are numerous, but first let us dispose well of its menace to safety. Where to put it is always a question: To stick it in a log or stump leaves one sharp edge flaring out. To place it on the ground exposes two edges to unsuspecting toes. To carry it on the shoulder is to threaten one's neck. To carry it in the hand may be to fall on it. It gets down to this: The double-bit belongs only in the hands of experienced users, whether boys, girls, or adults. In organized camps or other places where many people are about, it must be carefully guarded and used only by qualified campers. And it should always be muzzled with a sheath.

Then why use it at all? This chosen ax of the lumberjack, symbol of true woodsmanship, is easier to handle and to use than any other. It has better balance. Once accustomed to it, the single-bit seems awkward and clumsy. The weight of its head is in line with its cutting edge—it swings truer and bites deeper. But more: its two blades permit the keeping of one keen and thin for fine chopping, and the other thicker for use around knots or near the ground where a slip means a nick.

It is the small double-bit shown in D, Figure 88, that is important in camping—about a three-quarter size and carrying the title of the *cruiser ax*. It has a two-and-one-half pound head and a twenty-inch handle. The full double-bit in G with three-and-one-half-pound head is of little use in camp and is to be recommended only for jacks and woodsmen engaged regularly in felling. The cruiser size is light in weight, efficient in chopping, adequate for tree felling and all other uses in camp. It can be easily sheathed and if necessary can be carried on the belt. It is an excellent addition to the ax equipment of a qualified camper. This general style of ax is available from practically all of the ax manufacturers.

---

* See Nessmuk (Geo. W. Sears), *Woodcraft*, p. 11 (New York: Forest and Stream Publishing Company, 1884).

Single-Bit Axes.—There are many styles and weights of pole or single-bit axes, of which that in F, Figure 88, is typical, weighing three-and-one-half to four pounds with a helve thirty to thirty-one inches long. Excellent for splitting, it usually proves to be too large and clumsy for other purposes and finds little use in camp. For campers in their teens, and indeed preferred by most adults for camp use, the three-quarter ax with a two-and-one-half to three-pound head is recommended, or even the half ax with a two-pound head. And of the axes in this range, the *cedar ax* in E, Figure 88, has proven to be ideal for general camp use. Made originally for use in the cedar country, its wide blade resembling somewhat the Hudson Bay ax makes it an excellent chopping tool. And it is made to order for hewing and flattening logs. A very popular ax, and a good all-around one for camp.

Figure 89. AREA TO BE GROUND OR FILED IN SHARPENING

The Hudson Bay ax shown in C, Figure 88, is honored by long tradition in the North and is a good ax for rough country if only one ax can be taken, but would be less desirable than a pair consisting of a good hand-ax and a half or three-quarter ax. But some people like the Hudson Bay—it is a matter of taste.

Axes for the Trail.—Two, and perhaps three:

1. A good hand-ax, heavy enough to be of use. B, in Figure 88, is recommended.

2. A light double-bit of the cruiser model—D in Figure 88—provided the campers are qualified to use it. Otherwise a single-bit cedar ax or a three-quarter single-bit.

These will meet every emergency in any kind of country. If you must go light, just take the recommended hand-ax—it will get you by.

But if you aren't concerned about weight a *knock-about hatchet* of the type of A should be thrown in, making it three, for it will save your good axes—you might need to dig a trench for a fire!

Axes for Organized Camps.—If axmanship is to result from the camp experience, and let us hope it will, more is needed than the nicked-up, loose-helved pole-ax that the kitchen help uses to split stove wood! And more is needed than the hand or scout axes of the campers, essential as they are.

For the rank and file:

1. Hand-axes or scout axes—A in Figure 88—possessed by the campers.

2. Cedar axes for chopping, owned and made available by the camp—Figure 88.

For the more experienced:

1. Hand-axes with eighteen-inch handles—B in Figure 88.

2. Light-weight double-bits of the cruiser type in sheaths—D in Figure 88.

3. Single-bit cedar axes—Figure 88.

And the wood pile should possess a pole-ax with a three-and-one-half pound head for splitting—F in Figure 88.

Ax Handles

A loose helve is an abomination and a menace, yet sooner or later every ax reaches that condition, no matter how firm the handle may be as it comes from the factory. And how to keep it tight has always been a problem.

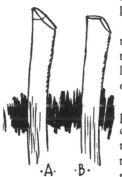

Soaking the ax in a pail of water will usually tighten a slightly loose helve but this is at best a temporary measure and the handle will be looser than ever when it dries. Rewedging is the only sure cure.

Wedging the Handle.—Remove the head and pry out the wedge. Make a new wedge of dry hardwood, long and slender, and evenly tapered. Wooden wedges are always better than metal ones. Replace the head and drive in the wedge as far as possible. Allow it to protrude a little, if possible, until the ax is used a while, then drive it again, and saw off flush.

·A·   ·B·

Figure 90.

The fawn-foot on the end of a single-bit handle makes it very difficult if not impossible to drive a helve into the eye of the ax. The term fawn-foot applies to the type of end seen in F, Figure 88. This is for appearance only, serving no useful purpose, and therefore the tip should be sawed off straight as in B, Figure 90, to produce a flat surface for driving the helve. The end thus produced fits the hand better anyway. It will be noted that the helve of the hand-ax in B,

Figure 88, is made with such a flat end. There is no fawn-foot on a double-bit ax, the helve always being straight.

Be sure the ax is hung so that the cutting edge is in exact line with the center of the handle as illustrated in Figure 91.

Removing a Broken Handle.—Tough to get out is a broken helve that is firmly wedged in the ax. Easiest to burn it out: if a single-bit, drive the blade in the ground and build a fire over it; if a double-bit dig a little ditch, lay the ax across it, pack dirt over the cutting edges, and build the fire. With the blade in the earth, there is no danger of the temper being ruined by the heat.

Making an Ax Handle.—When a helve breaks in the woods there is no choice but to make a new one. Don't attempt a curved handle—it is hard to do and wholly unnecessary for a straight handle does as well, and indeed is preferred by many even on a pole-ax. Use sound hickory, white oak, ash or elm. Cut a five-inch log to a length slightly greater than the desired handle, quarter it, and chop out and discard the core wood from one of the sections. Chop the stick down roughly to the shape of the handle and finish the shaping with a crooked knife (see Chapter XIII). The handle should now be dried by suspending it in the sun for three or four days by means of a string tied to one end. Then sand it smooth, split the end, and wedge in the ax as already described.

Figure 91.

AX IN
LINE WITH
HANDLE

PUTTING MAGIC IN IT

A new ax needs grinding before it is used.

Spotless and shining as it comes from the store, one is inclined to assume that it is in first-class chopping trim, but not so! for the manufacturer left the blade wide and blunt, not knowing to what use the purchaser would want to put it. This is particularly true of a full-sized ax. As it stands it is in good form for *splitting* firewood, but not for chopping, because splitting requires a wide and stunt blade whereas chopping demands a thin and keen one. Since a camper will want a chopping ax primarily, the ax should be thinned down from a point three inches back from the blade up to a half inch from it or to where the bevel of the blade starts. This should be done on a grindstone with plenty of water and not on a power wheel which will destroy its temper. *Have it done by an expert who knows his business.*

Once put in shape this grinding will never need to be done again if the ax is occasionally sharpened with a file.

Sharpening.—Using a file for the purpose, the ax should be sharpened every few days to keep it thin and in working order. Lay the ax on the ground with the blade standing upward and resting against a stick, and, steadying it with the left hand, place the file against the flat of the blade and push away from the edge. Start the filing a half inch from the edge or at the beginning of the bevel, and always shove away from the blade so as not to bring the file in contact with the edge. Keep the ax wet. File both edges uniformly with the rough side of the file, and then repeat with the fine side. If it is a double-bit, drive one blade in a log to hold secure while working on the other.

Now for the honing of the edge: Place the carborundum stone against the bevel of the cutting edge and move it with a circular motion from the middle of the ax up to the edge. Then reverse the ax and hone the other side to remove the wire edge the first process created. Remember the ax must be kept moist. Filing is necessary only every few days, but honing is important each time the ax is used if it is to be kept in perfect trim.

Use Your Own Ax

It is bad taste to ask a man to lend you his ax. In the woods an ax is considered a personal tool. It is hard enough at best to keep it in first-class shape, and no one wants to risk having it come back with a saw edge, a loose head, or a chewed-up helve. Don't ask to borrow it, and if you do, expect to be refused. And if refused, it is no reflection on friendship. It just isn't done.

And conversely, don't lend your ax. Get a good one, keep it in shape, and let the other man use his own.

And this means that you must keep it where the other fellow can't help himself, which he is dead certain to do every time he sees it whether or not he has use for it. That is a weakness to which all humankind seems to be given—a person just can't walk past an ax without picking it up, taking a whack or two at something with it, and throwing it down. And for no apparent reason other than to relieve the itching in his hands which the sight of an ax always seems to create.

DANGER

Of course the ax is dangerous—every sharp-edged tool is. And the better the ax the greater the hazard. Most accidents happen to the foolhardy. You can't be too careful, especially when learning. A boy's beginning days should always be under the guidance of an adult who knows—then he will learn rapidly and with safety.

1. The ax should always be stuck in a stump or log during rest periods, never leaned against a tree or dropped on the ground. But do not leave it stuck long or it will sweat and become dull—put it in its sheath.

2. If it's a double-bit, stick it *under* a log.

3. Indoors, lay the ax on the floor, blade to the wall.

4. If it's a double-bit, set it up in a corner with the two blades touching the walls.

5. In carrying an ax on the shoulder, hold the blade away from you.

6. A double-bit should never be carried unless it is muzzled. The light double-bits acceptable for camping can easily be sheathed.

7. If you fall, throw the ax.

8. All brush, vines, and debris should be cleared before chopping. Right here is the cause of most serious accidents. Take time to clear *everything* within reach as far as you can swing the ax in all directions.

9. An ax with a loose helve should *never* be used.

10. When a tree falls, the chopper should stand to one side, never behind it—more on this later.

USING THE TWO-HANDED AX

Chopping, hewing, splitting, trimming, and felling—these are the essential arts of axmanship. Assuming we are using an ax that must be handled with two hands, rather than a hatchet, let us consider the knacks of each art.

CHOPPING

Three basic principles:

First, *a log should be chopped with the axman standing on top of it and cutting through it from its sides* as illustrated in C, Figure 92. Most beginners want to stand to one side and chop the top of the log, with the result that by the time they are halfway through they are in a jam, for the V has been carried as far as possible and the log is too heavy to be turned over to get at the other side. See A, Figure 92 —it shows the right and wrong way; and B shows the appearance of the proper cut as you look down at the top of the log while standing on it—it has been chopped halfway through on one side, then on the other side.

Second, *only blows struck at an angle bite into the log.* D in Figure 92 shows it: to swing straight at the log cuts no wood—the rebound prevents the force from counting, the cross-grain permits no more than a shallow dent, and worst of all, the ax becomes dulled. At an angle of forty-five degrees to the log or a little more, the ax takes hold. And the cut thus made permits the removing of the chips necessary to sever the log. *But beware of glancing blows:* An ax swung at less than forty-five degrees may not bite into the log at all but may glance off and swing up dangerously, especially if gripped so loosely as to permit the handle to twist in the hand. Often such a glancing blow will carry the ax right out of the hand just as a baseball player's bat sometimes gets away as he swings.

Third, *good chopping is gentle chopping.* Never ride the ax or force it. It is the weight of the ax that chops, not the force with which it is swung. To drive the ax is hard work, and wholly unnecessary work. But worse—it destroys your aim. Accuracy is what counts in chopping. A good sharp ax will eat its way through a log quickly and cleanly if raised and dropped with a normal, natural, unforced, rhythmic swing. Such chopping will always score for speed over a violent display of strength.

Width of the Notch.—The commonest mistake is to make the notch too narrow, with the result that before the center of the log is reached the V is so pinched that chips cannot be removed, and the chopper must start again with a wider notch.

The notch should be as wide as the log itself—that is the safe rule for beginners. It errs a little on the wide side, for with experienced choppers the notch may be slightly less than the width—a ten-inch log would require a notch about eight inches wide; an eighteen-inch log a notch about fifteen to sixteen inches wide.

Mark the edges of the notch before you start to chop.

Chopping Form.—Grasp the handle with the left hand two or three inches from the end and hold it with the right hand near the head, about three-quarters of the way up the handle. Raise it up over the

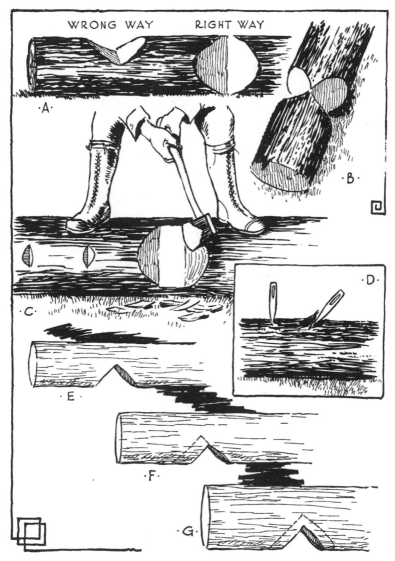

WRONG WAY   RIGHT WAY

·A·

·B·

·C·

·D·

·E·

·F·

·G·

Figure 92.

right shoulder with the hands in this position, then as you swing it down to the log let the right hand slide down naturally until it touches the left. Most boys want to swing the ax as a baseball bat, with hands together, but easy, accurate, efficient chopping demands that the right hand should slide up and down with each swing.

First, *the forehand swing:* Mount the log as described, weight evenly divided on both feet. Bend your head well down to look at the log. Raise the ax up over the right shoulder with hands in the position described. Swing it down, sliding the right hand down the handle as you do so. The ax should cut into the log at an angle of forty-five degrees to the log or a little more. Then swing it back up and repeat. Usually three chops are made on the right side of the cut before shifting to the left, one near the top of the log, the second near the bottom, and the third in the middle. A slight twist should be given the helve just as it strikes to prevent it from sticking or freezing fast.

Now *the backhand swing:* Having made the three chops on the right side as directed, we are ready to start on the left side of the notch. Here position changes slightly; shift the weight to the left leg and lean to the left enough to clear the way for the ax. Raise the ax over the right shoulder as before, hands holding the ax as usual, and swing down sending the ax into the log at the usual angle but entering it on the left side of the notch. Here three strokes are needed also— first, high; second, low; third, in the middle. Remember to twist the helve a little just as the ax hits to throw out the chips.

This is the routine—three chops on the right side of the notch, three on the left, three on the right again, and so on until the notch reaches a point at the center of the log. Of course, if one's aim is bad and one of the chops is ineffective, more than three will be needed on each side.

Keep your eye on the spot on the log and put the ax there. It is just as important to "keep your eye on the ball" in chopping as it is in batting in baseball. Chop gently, with your mind on swinging true rather than swinging hard.

The notch halfway through, turn around and start the notch on the other side, continuing until the second notch meets the first and the log is severed.

Chopping Large Logs.—We have assumed thus far that the log is a foot or less in diameter. Of such size, the necessary notch is not too wide but that the chips can be thrown out easily by chopping a straight V as in E, Figure 92. Larger logs require notches so wide that the chips cannot be removed if we attempt the V at its full width. Therefore, we must make a notch not over a foot in width and then widen it later. There are two ways to do this, depending on the size of the log.

If the log is between a foot and eighteen inches, cut a notch ten to twelve inches wide, and when the V has been brought down to a point enlarge it on one side as indicated by the dotted lines in F, Figure 92. If the log is wider than that make the twelve-inch notch as usual, then enlarge it on *both* sides as indicated in G.

Chopping Small Poles.—If you would ruin your ax, lay the poles on the ground and chop them into firewood lengths—even though the ax hits no rocks to chip it, the unavoidable contact with the earth will surely take off the edge.

Lay the pole over a log as in A, Figure 93, and strike a slanting blow with the ax as shown. Tilt the ax over as it strikes to throw the

Figure 93. CHOPPING SMALL POLES

cut end of the stick down. But be sure that the ax hits over the point where the stick rests solidly on the log, or you will send it whirling in the air, probably in your face. B in Figure 93 shows what is apt to happen if you cut it between the log and the ground. I know an old woodsman who has gone through life with one eye owing to such a foolish stroke during his boyhood days.

If the sapling is not too large, hold it in the left hand across the log and cut with a slanting blow at the point of contact. But be sure you hit it directly over the point where it rests on the log or it will stun your left arm most disagreeably.

HEWING

To flatten a log as is often necessary in making rustic furniture and in log construction, the log must be scored and hewed as in

Figure 94. In order that the flat area may be straight, a chalk line should be used—hence the term "hewing to a line." Blacken the chalk line with charcoal and fasten one end in a nick cut in the log. Stretch the line straight down the log and then attach the other end in a nick. Now snap the line and remove it to find a black guide line on the log. Repeat on the other side.

Score the log with a series of notches as in B, then chop out the wood between the notches to produce the flat top as in D. If the log is not too big and you are handy with the ax, perhaps you can score it by a series of cuts as in C rather than notches.

The ideal ax for flattening a log in this way is one with a broad and thin blade, and woodsmen frequently have a special ax for the purpose. The light cedar ax recommended earlier in this chapter has a blade that is unusually satisfactory for the purpose—another point in its favor as a good all-around camp ax.

Of course the best tool for hewing is an *adz* but this is a rare item nowadays and dangerous always in the hands of the inexperienced.

SPLITTING

Split firewood we must, and often, and sometimes we must split a full-sized log in half.

Splitting Firewood.—Cut to stovewood length and set on end, a good whack with the ax will sever the chunk in twain unless it be a stubborn wood or one with a knot in it. In which case a wedge roughly made must be driven into the crack started by the ax as illustrated in A, Figure 95.

Always give the ax a slight twist just as the blade hits the chunk in order to free it from sticking fast and to pry open the crack—this is a good knack to get and use in all kinds of chopping.

The chunk split in half, there are two ways to reduce it to stovewood. The way of the expert is to lean it against a block, and standing on the far side of the block, to split it as indicated in B, Figure 95. More commonly seen is to stand on the near side and put your toe on the end of the chunk to hold it while you whack away as suggested in C, but this method is without regard for your toes. Do it the other way and play safe.

If you have a permanent wood pile that is the scene of frequent chopping, a *chopping block* is a great convenience. This is a Y-shaped contraption, made from the crotch of a six-inch tree, as shown in D,

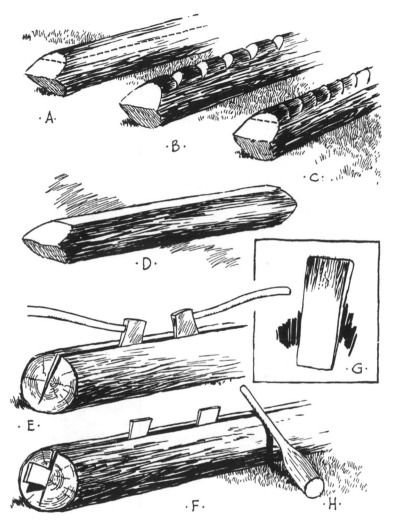

Figure 94. HEWING AND SPLITTING

Figure 95. Install the chunk in the crotch as shown and stand behind the butt of the block to chop it. To make a better one, use an eight-inch log for the Y and flatten the top by hewing it down to present a flat surface for cutting kindling and small stuff. It goes without saying that this block should be of tough wood.

Figure 95. SPLITTING FIREWOOD

Splitting Logs.—Like spokes of a wheel the medullary rays radiate from the center of a log, obvious to the eye at a glance. These are the natural lines of cleavage, and the lines along which splitting should be done. Study the end of the log—sometimes a larger crack exists that indicates at once the easiest splitting course.

Two axes will split a log if it is not too large and tough. Drive one ax in the side of the log near the end and drive the second ax in the same crack a few inches farther along with its handle in the opposite direction, as shown in E, Figure 94. The second ax frees the first which is withdrawn and driven in again farther down the log, repeating the process until the split has been carried the entire length.

But if you have much splitting to do or are tackling a big log, iron wedges will be appreciated. Without them you will have to make gluts or wooden wedges, for which apple or ironwood are best—select a young sapling and flatten the two sides equally to wedge shape, then cut off the end to a square for pounding, as shown in G, Figure 94. Make the wedges plenty long and give care to sloping the sides uniformly.

A *maul* or *beetle* must also be fashioned for driving the wedges, whether iron or wood, for no ax should be struck against an iron wedge, and pounding with an ax will ruin a wooden glut. Club-shaped as illustrated in H, Figure 94, the maul is made of tough hardwood such as ironwood or hickory. Select a young sapling five to six inches in diameter and chop it off as low as possible since the wood is toughest near the roots. Cut off a section of the butt two-and-one-half feet long, leave the lower third of it at its full width, and trim down the remainder for the handle as shown.

Always start the splitting at the small end of the log. First drive the ax in the end by pounding it with the maul until a crack is started, into which one or two wedges or gluts are driven as illustrated in F, Figure 94. This will split the log on the side near the end, into which crack a wedge is driven. The crack is then continued the full length of the log by driving wedges at intervals, using the ax when necessary to produce a crack wide enough to accommodate the wedges. Force the wedges deeper and deeper until the log splits. *Never drive an iron wedge with an ax, nor an ax with another ax.*

Slabs for the making of lean-tos and for the walls of shacks may be split by the use of wedges in this way, and in like fashion are produced the floor-boards or *puncheons* of the pioneer cabins. The simplest way is to split small logs in half and use them as they are without further splitting. But to secure wide slabs or puncheons from large logs, first split in half and then split each section again parallel to the flat side. But there is woe aplenty in this second splitting unless it happens to be an easily splittable log. Some woods split very easily, as for example ash, cedar or chestnut, but individual logs of the same kind vary greatly—in determining this matter the nose of an experienced woodsman is more to be trusted than any formula or description.

Trimming Off Branches

In "swamping" or lopping off branches from a down tree, start at the butt and work to the top, cutting from the underside of the branches, *never in the crotch*. To whack in the crotch is to rip off the branch and a good supply of bark below it, which must in turn be cut with a second swing of the ax. It is a pretty big branch that cannot be lopped off closely and cleanly by one swing of the ax from underneath. In the logging camps the swampers use a special "swamping ax," a double-bit with thin blades which cleans up a tree for the snakers in short order.

In trimming a branch from a standing tree it is often difficult to cut from beneath, especially if it is far over one's head, but the bark at least should be severed on the underside before striking into the crotch—otherwise the bark will be ripped off down the side of the tree, leaving an ugly and wholly unnecessary scar.

Beware of hemlock and balsam knots—they will chip the best ax made.

Felling a Tree

There is danger in felling a tree. It is a feat for experienced hands and should never be undertaken by a boy except under adult guidance.

First off, determine where you are going to drop it, which involves three factors—the lean of the tree, the surroundings, and the wind. If at all possible drop it in the direction toward which the wind is blowing. Practically every tree leans somewhat or has heavier foliage on one side, and other things being equal, it should be dropped in the direction of the lean. If it must fall into other trees, select the direction where the trees are small or your tree may become "hung" and that is bad, for no one short of an expert can free a hung tree with anything approaching safety.

Now to drop it in the selected direction: First cut the notch on the side of the tree towards which it is to fall, as indicated by the arrow in A, Figure 96. This notch is to extend halfway through the tree and therefore its width is half the thickness of the log. Assuming that our tree is a foot in diameter the notch would be six inches wide. Figure out the width of the kerf or notch and mark it on the tree before starting to chop. Note that the bottom of the notch is chopped flat, or level with the ground, and that the upper side of it is at an angle of forty-five degrees. The stump left by a beginner often looks as though a beaver had chewed it off—start the notch full six inches in width and take out big chips. This first notch completed, start the second notch on the back of the tree, directly opposite the first but two or three inches higher. This notch is also made with a flat bottom. Very little chopping will be necessary here before the tree will go toppling down in the direction of the first cut.

As soon as you hear a crack or see that the tree begins to shudder and sway, *step to one side and stay there. Never stand behind a fall-*

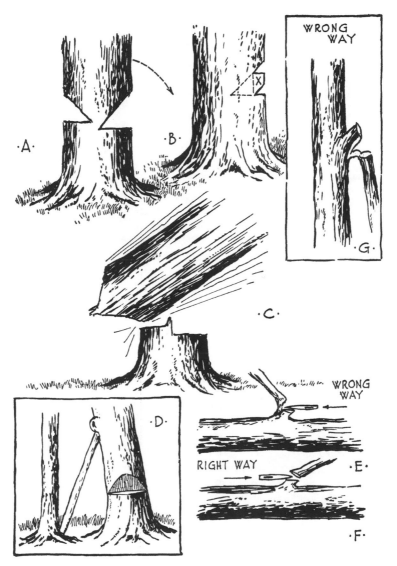

Figure 96.

ing tree for it may kick back and if it does it will come with the speed of lightning—once kicked, you will never chop another tree! And never run away from the tree—the safe place is a few feet to one side.

Given a tree larger than a foot in diameter, the notch necessary to drop it will be of such width that it cannot be chopped as described, because the chips cannot be easily removed from a simple notch that is wider than six inches. To negotiate such a tree, mark the width of the notch—half the diameter of the log—and start two notches as shown in B, Figure 96, one above the other, and then knock out the block marked X between them. Continue thus until the notch is of such width that normal chopping can be accomplished.

In chopping the notch, the same process is followed as already described for chopping a down log in two: Starting at the bottom of the notch, first chop on the far side of the tree, then on the near side, and finally in the middle—three cuts in all. Then repeat at the top of the notch, first on the far side, then on the near side, and lastly in the middle. This assumes of course that all chops are well directed and effective, otherwise more than three will be needed. The side chops should be far enough to the side so that the outer point of the ax blade does not bite the wood. This method prevents the ax from sticking fast in the tree. With each swing give the ax a slight twist just as it hits not only to prevent it from freezing in the wood but also to pry loose the chips.

If there is a strong wind blowing contrariwise, better wait for a calmer and safer day. A slight sidewise wind should be taken into consideration in cutting the notch, for the foliage catches the wind like a sail and may tip the tree where you do not want it.

If the tree has a sidewise lean, the direction of the notch will again be altered slightly. It is sometimes possible to offset a slight sideward lean by a brace against the tree as shown in D, Figure 96.

Standing six feet from the main lodge of a boys' camp and leaning badly over it, a large sugar maple had to be dropped for the safety of the building. The owner decided to risk it only in the hands of a dependable old woodsman. With squinting eyes but otherwise immovable features the old-timer looked it over and finally said curtly that he would be back and tip it over. Impatient as the days went by the owner sought the woodsman but got no more than a promise that he'd get to it soon. Came the day at long last when the woodsman arrived ax in hand and promptly and neatly laid the tree down directly away from the building. The owner voiced his relief with many compliments but told him it took him too blamed long to get at it. Whereat the woodsman retorted that if the owner had ever cut a tree that was leaning like that, he would know that he had to wait for the right wind to blow it over!

Better wait for the wind, but a tree with a pretty bad lean can be felled in the opposite direction by putting a block of wood in the back notch and driving a wedge under it. Square off the top of the notch so the block will have a square shoulder on which to rest, and fit the block snugly but leave sufficient room for the tip of the wedge to be inserted beneath. A definite lean can be offset in this way but it is safer to assist a good woodsman the first time you undertake such a feat.

And lastly, *beware of "sailors."* These are broken branches, on trees struck by falling timber, which remained in the trees at the time, and later come hurtling down without warning.

USING THE HATCHET

Big or little, it is an ax and deserves respect and good treatment. All that has been said on caring for the ax applies equally to the young-sized hand-ax.

Cut to firewood length, chunks of wood up to five inches in diameter can be readily split with a hand-ax by pounding it into the end of the block with a piece of wood as in A, Figure 97. Do this with a stick, however, and not another ax.

In order to split small stuff, place the blade of the ax lengthwise of the stick as in B, Figure 97, and bring both ax and stick down together on a log. This is safer and surer of success than to lay the stick on the log and swing the ax down at it.

Similarly, to cut small poles and branches to firewood length, hold the pole in the left hand and place the ax crosswise on it, then bring both down together on to the log as in C, Figure 97. In chopping larger poles the previously stated rules for the width of the notch apply.

In trimming twigs off small branches, hold the butt of the stick in the hand and slide the ax down along it, striking the branches from the underside.

All of these methods prevent the ax from coming in contact with the ground. Never work on or near the ground with a hand-ax for as surely as you do the cutting edge will be gone.

One can whittle with an ax as efficiently as with a knife, provided of course its blade is keen, as it should be. Shavings and fuzzed-up sticks for lighting the campfire are always done with the ax. Just

Figure 97. USING THE CAMP-AX

grasp the poll or back of the ax in the heel of the hand and proceed to whittle.

AXMANSHIP CONTESTS

The logging rodeo finds the jacks in sportive mood. Log-chopping contests, loading and unloading contests, burling and log-rolling contests*—the big-muscled and brawny descendants of Paul Bunyan vie with one another in the time-honored skills of the timber country—contests much loved by all who follow the woodcraft way.

But from the red woodsmen instead of the lumberjacks we get the most joyous of ax sports—tomahawk throwing.

LOG-CHOPPING CONTESTS †

From the expert to the youthful beginner, this contest is challenging as a test of skill in a manly art. But make the preparations

---

* For a full description of how to roll or burl a log, and the contests used in log-rolling, see Bernard S. Mason, *Primitive and Pioneer Sports*, Chapter XVIII (New York: A. S. Barnes and Company, 1937).

† For this and similar woodcraft contests see Bernard S. Mason and Elmer D. Mitchell, *Social Games for Recreation*, Chapter XVI (New York: A. S. Barnes and Company, 1935).

carefully: A log twelve to sixteen inches in diameter is suitable for men, eight to twelve inches for boys. Saw into sections two-and-one-half feet long, and trim the larger pieces down to the diameter of the smallest. Each chopping log should be mounted on two crosswise poles five inches in diameter, with braces nailed on the ends as clearly shown in Figure 98. The contestants in each heat should be given sections of the same log. It is permissible to cut footholds near the

Figure 98. Log Prepared for Chopping Contest

ends of the log if desired, but any marks used to indicate the width of the notches for the chopping must be put on with crayon and not made with the ax.

At the starting gun the choppers lay to and the one wins who first has his log cleanly cut with the two pieces resting on the ground. If conducted in heats, the winners compete in the final.

Tomahawk Throwing

I have already set forth in complete and full detail in another book the various methods of throwing a tomahawk, the many types of throws, and the contests used in this glorious sport.*

The Scout ax of the type shown in A, Figure 88, is the ideal throwing ax. At five steps (not paces) away from the dead tree, it will revolve once and stick. Stand at this distance, your feet squarely on the ground with the left toe slightly in advance of the right, and grip the ax in your hand as near the end of the handle as possible. Then hold it upright in front of you and steady it with the left hand, keeping it straight up and down, tilted neither to the right nor left. Remove the left hand, draw the ax back without tilting, and throw it

---

* See Bernard S. Mason, *Primitive and Pioneer Sports*, Chapter XVII (New York: A. S. Barnes and Company, 1937).

straight at the log with a downward motion of the arm, at the same time stepping forward with the left foot. It will make one revolution and stick. The knack will come with time, but if the ax seems to behave right yet does not stick, experiment by changing the distance from the log a few inches until the proper throwing point for you is found.

There are many ways of throwing an ax, and many distances at which it may be thrown, for which the book just referred to should be consulted.

Tomahawk throwing is fun but like all feats involving an ax there is an element of danger involved. *Be careful.* Always stand behind the man who is throwing, not to one side of him. The ax may rebound from the tree or glance off from it. The man having thrown, allow him to retrieve his ax and return before you take the throwing line. *You cannot be too careful!*

USING THE SAW

Ax and saw—companion tools of the backwoods, they go hand in hand in the work-a-day life of the lumberjack and should be so related in the woodcraft life of boys. Handy by the woodpile of the boys' camp should be a *bucksaw, a crosscut saw*, and a *cedar saw* or *half saw*, these to be used in the training of campers who will be efficient alike with ax and saw.

THE BUCKSAW

Sawing branches, poles, and small stuff to stove-wood length is the function of the bucksaw. The sawbuck which supports the pole while being sawed is shown in A, Figure 99—the height of the crotch should be about sixteen inches so that when the pole is in place it will be of convenient height to be steadied by the knee or foot. Eighteen to twenty inches is a good width because a narrow buck is more convenient than a wide one.

THE CROSSCUT SAW

An expert with the ax is developed only after years of practice, but anyone can become proficient with the crosscut saw in short order. There is just one thing to remember: Your job is to pull the saw toward you and to help to guide it, *not to push it back.* The beginner, anxious to help in every way he can, shoves back as lustily

Figure 99. SAWBUCKS

as he pulls with the result that he buckles the saw on the back push, and hinders rather than helps the man on the other end. This is called "riding the saw" and is certain to draw the ire of your partner.

There are two main types of sawbucks used for the crosscut saw, the commonest and the handiest being shown in C, Figure 99. Two poles are needed, each five or six inches in diameter and ten or twelve feet long. Into one end bore two diagonal holes in which the legs are inserted as illustrated, bringing one end of the pole up to a height of about three feet. The holes for these legs go only part way through the log, and the legs are whittled to fit, the ends split, and a wedge inserted before they are driven in; the wedge tightens as it hits the end of the bore to hold the leg fast—see D in Figure 99. At intervals of every foot throughout the length of the pole, holes are bored to accommodate the upright pins for holding the log in position—this is clearly illustrated in the drawing. The happy feature of this kind of a sawbuck is that the log may be easily rolled up into position, one man being able to hoist an average-sized log without help. When the log is at the desired height, merely insert a pin in the nearest hole below it to prevent it from rolling down. Sometimes only one of these bucks is used as in B, but it is handier to use two.

The other type of sawbuck for the crosscut saw is made from a half log with legs inserted in the bottom after the pattern of a slab bench—E in Figure 99 illustrates it. The pegs extending out of the top to hold the log secure are extensions of the legs—the leg holes are drilled clear through, the legs whittled to fit and driven in as illustrated in F, with wedges of wood inserted at the sides if necessary to take up the play. Two additional pegs are then inserted near the middle as shown. Often the whole logs are used for this sawbuck rather than split logs. The chief difficulty with this kind of a sawbuck is that it takes two men to hoist the log into position, whereas one man can usually manipulate the first type without assistance.

THE CEDAR SAW

The cedar saw is a one-man saw, resembling the crosscut saw in all respects except that it is about half its length and has a handle on one end only. It is a handy and extremely useful tool in the woods, making it possible for one man to cut logs of average size as readily as he saws small stuff with the bucksaw. Trees may be felled with it, too—in fact the felling of cedar and other soft woods is the chief use to which it is put in the logging camps. To the loggers cutting in the evergreen areas, the cedar saw is as important a part of their equipment as the ax. This saw is much loved by boys in camp who find it easily within their capacity. It is an ideal tool to have around.

One of the sawbucks recommended in the preceding section should be constructed for the cedar saw, preferably the one with sloping supports because one man works alone with this saw and the sloping poles of this buck permit him to hoist the logs unassisted.

Felling Trees with a Saw

First, cut a small notch three or four inches deep on the side towards which you want the tree to fall. Then start the sawing from the opposite side, beginning three or four inches above the notch and slanting the cut down to meet it. The saw will not go far into the tree before it begins to bind severely, making further progress impossible, which situation calls for a wedge driven into the crack on the back side. If the saw binds again, drive the wedge in farther. The wedge not only loosens the crack enough to facilitate sawing but it also tilts the tree in the desired direction.

As the moment becomes imminent for the tree to topple, one man withdraws the handle at his end of the crosscut saw and steps aside, allowing the other man to complete the task. As soon as the tree begins to crack, the saw is withdrawn and both step to one side. One man can easily fell softwood trees with the cedar saw.

Crosscut-Sawing Contests

The best way to conduct a crosscut-sawing contest is against time, using a stopwatch and keeping the time of each contestant, then comparing the times to determine the winner. A log of uniform width throughout is needed. Place the log on supports and have each contestant saw off a six-inch section of the end. The sawing starts with the crack of a gun and the time is taken when the sawed-off section hits the ground.*

Parbuckling a Log

One has a problem on his hands if he must move a log single-handed as he is frequently called upon to do in getting it into position for

---

* For this and similar contests, see Bernard S. Mason and Elmer D. Mitchell, *Social Games for Recreation.* Chapter XVI. (New York: A. S. Barnes and Company, 1935.)

sawing. Given a cant-hook the log can be turned over and can even be rolled some distance laboriously, but an old-fashioned parbuckle will remove it in a fraction of the time, and with only one man to do the pulling at that.

Figure 100 shows the set up. A long rope is needed which is doubled

Figure 100. PARBUCKLE

around a stump or tree. The ends are then slipped under the ends of the log as shown, and doubled back over the top. By pulling on the ends the log can be rolled easily and with surprisingly little effort.

Parbuckles were used in the old days to hoist heavy barrels up a gangway onto a wagon. One man on the wagon could easily bring up a barrel so heavy that several men could not lift it outright.